Diary of a Mid-Li

by

Jane Cullen

Copyright © 2019 Jane Cullen

ISBN: 978-0-244-52131-8

PublishNation
www.publishnation.co.uk

Acknowledgements

Special mention must go to the following:

Peak Tours and your amazing adventure holidays. If I hadn't tripped over your website, I might never have had the courage to set off in the first place. Your tour guides had a huge impact on my journeys, and I will forever remember Isabelle, Alberto and Dylan.

My fellow cyclists. Thank you for the banter and support on all of my trips, but especially to Debbie from C2C, Phil and John from LeJog, and Trevor and Vicky from C2M. My rides would have been very different without you.

My brothers and sisters. You have all always been an inspiration to me. I couldn't have been the runt of a better litter!

Cameron, Rebecca and James. We're looking forward to following the next chapter in your exciting lives. We burst with pride on a daily basis.

Mum and Dad. Thank you for teaching us all the true meaning of the word 'family'.

Bob. You have been by my side with your unfailing love and encouragement since the day we met. I would be lost without you.

Prologue

On 10 May 2014, I boarded a train heading south – a long way south. My destination was Land's End, and my plan was to cycle northwards for 1000 miles, the entire length of the UK. I was almost 47 years old, very happily married with two grown up children, but I had just ripped off my comfort blanket and was about to do something completely out of character. Two weeks and a huge adventure later I arrived at John O'Groats, tired and in tears, but determined that this wouldn't be a one-off. I promised myself that for my 50th I would embark on another challenge, and this time cycle the length of France from the Channel to the Med. I had three years to get the money and motivation together, but my goal was set, I was focussed, and there was nothing standing in my way! I could never have predicted the epic shift that was about to hit, so in the meantime I simply sat back, enjoyed wallowing in the enormity of my achievement, and took stock of how I'd come to this point in my life.

Years 1 to 45

Mine had not been a remarkable life. I had what I consider to be a 'normal' upbringing, although everyone's perceptions of normal differ greatly. For me, life started in a house just outside Manchester city centre, with a lovely Mum and Dad, four older siblings, lots of wider family living close by, and plenty of pals at the local school. Our house was the hub for all our friends and was always noisy, but it was happy noise, and all five of us look back fondly on our childhoods.

Dad was a self-employed plumber, working very hard to provide, but he was also the mainstay of the household. He was a big man, strong, with a deep booming voice, but he was the very essence of the gentle giant. Unlike many Dads of that era, he was very hands-on with all of us, and to him, family was everything. It was Dad we went to if we were poorly in the night, Dad who read our bedtime stories, and Dad who took us all to our various after-school activities.

Mum was equally hard-working, and quietly she was the strength of the family through our early years. Although she'd had a number of jobs, my memory of her as I was growing up was as homemaker - cooking, cleaning, sewing, and keeping the peace. This was no mean feat with five of us spread through an age gap of 13 years, all with very differing personalities. Times must have been hard for them financially, but we were never aware of this, and we all had new clothes (albeit handmade!), plenty of good home baking, and a house full of music, fun and laughter.

Mum and Dad were a strong couple, both from large close-knit families themselves, and from a very young age we were all taught the importance of family bond and community spirit. Our early years were a blur of schools, Brownies, Guides, Boys' Brigade, dancing and music lessons, with an annual camping holiday thrown in every summer. Ours was a very contented childhood.

By the time I reached my mid-teens I became more self-conscious, feeling I needed to 'fit in', and I went through a rebellious phase causing Mum and Dad much heartache. I'm not proud of what I put them through, but thankfully it was short-lived, and by 19 I was pretty stable, in work, with my own car and motorbike.

I had watched my brothers and sisters grow up and leave home, all very successful in their own fields, mostly married and living fairly close by, and I could see my life was heading in the same direction. I felt a little suffocated in our Manchester cocoon, and worried that there was a big world out there, which I might never get to see. If I'm honest, there's still a very big world out there that I haven't yet seen, and it's not that I didn't want the happy lifestyle with 2.4 kids. It was just that I fancied a challenge - something a bit less 'ordinary'. So, inspired by a college tutor who had recalled tales of her time in the services, I walked into the local RAF recruiting office, and announced that I wanted to be a Fighter Controller, just like she had been. I had no idea of what that really entailed, and no concept of how difficult a job it might be, but I quite liked the sound of it…

There quickly followed various selection processes, interviews, aptitude and fitness tests; and then the letter arrived telling me my application had been successful. Although Mum and Dad were very supportive, I'm still not entirely sure whether they were happy that I'd joined up, but I know they were the proudest parents on the parade ground when I graduated as a Pilot Officer, and set off to learn how to be a Fighter Controller.

It turns out that Fighter Control is a lot harder than I had anticipated! I was very much a rabbit in the headlights at first, sitting in front of a radar screen and talking to fast jet pilots over the radio, but after four months of intense graft, knock-backs and tears, I managed to pass the course at the first attempt. Actually, the job mostly required the right aptitude, and the sort of brain that can remember numbers and which works logically, and I do have a very orderly and methodical mind. So there I was, just turned 20 and living the dream, but now in the knowledge that the reality of the 'dream' was a tiring shift pattern, a very stressful job, and responsibility pushing the limits of my ability. Maybe I should've done a little more research into Fighter Control, but at least I'd had the foresight to only sign up for a short time, a total of four years from graduation. Having said that, those four years were some of the best times of my life, and I had a ball!

It took me a little while to get used to being away from home. Up to now I hadn't seen much of the outside world, barely venturing far from my Manchester bubble, and I didn't even have a passport! To date, all of my friends had come from a similar background to me, and mine had been a sheltered life. But now I was living and working with all kinds of people – some had been to boarding school, most to university, and they seemed to have such tales to tell of their exciting lives and fancy holidays. I was just a little lass from Manchester, way out of my depth socially, and I felt inferior and a bit overwhelmed. But it didn't take long to realise that they weren't any better than me - just different. I felt incredibly fortunate to have had the comparatively boring but blissfully happy childhood I had enjoyed, and although they may have seen and done more things than I had, I probably had a much better grounding than a lot of them. I soon relaxed into my new life, and fitted in well.

I was lucky to have travelled widely with the RAF, seeing many places in the UK which I'd never been to before, and also spending short spells abroad. Belize was most definitely the highpoint of my RAF adventure. By then I had spent six months in Cyprus, working hard, playing hard, and enjoying all that life by the Mediterranean can offer. At the other end of the scale, I spent four months in the Falklands, whose barren beauty and wonderful wildlife had provided the main distraction from being snowed-in on a remote mountain top accessible only by helicopter.

I had become used to seeing the 'unusual' but Belize was something very different. This was my first (and to date, my only) trip to the Caribbean, and one which will live with me forever. I visited real-life desert islands which we took water-taxis to, snorkelled in coral reefs with fish I'd only seen at the zoo, trekked through the jungle on horseback, cooling off under waterfalls, and explored ancient Mayan ruins across the border in Guatemala. I was only there for two months, but I felt like Judith Chalmers on 'Wish You Were Here', experiencing things that girls like me don't normally have the chance to see or do. Who would believe that I had been to remote villages in the heart of a rainforest with the army medical team, pulling teeth and performing minor surgery on some of the local Belizean people who had walked for days to be seen by the 'English Doctors'? I have the photos to prove it!

But it was in Cyprus that I met my future husband. Bob was a bit older than me, and several ranks above. I had only just arrived on the island when a few of us were invited from our radar station at the top of Mount Olympus, to an Octoberfest party at the main RAF base at Akrotiri, a couple of hours drive down the mountain. I set off with the others, suitably attired, and was soon swept away in an evening of beer, brass bands, and drinking games. I was also swept away by Bob, and although the details of that evening are a little 'hazy' to say the least, we certainly seemed to have 'chemistry'. The following few months were a whirlwind, with my work up the mountain, the vicious winter with 23 feet of snow, and the holiday romance with Bob whenever I could spend my days off down the mountain by the coast with him. Bob and I both liked to party, and we lived life to the full when we were together, having a short but exhilarating 'fling' before my six-month stint was up and I was to return to the UK, clutching happy memories of my time by the Med.

That was when I realised that this was more than a holiday romance after all. I missed Bob. I wanted to call him each evening to tell him how my day had gone. I longed to hear his soft Scottish lilt, and when I closed my eyes I could still see his smile and feel his warmth. But this was the 80's - there were no mobile phones or internet, and we had to make do with good old-fashioned letters. It might sound odd, but I think that in writing, our friendship turned into something intimately special. There's so much more you can convey on paper. You take time to really think about what you're about to say, and I spent hours reading and re-reading his replies.

Two years of long-distance romance later, and we found ourselves on back-to-back deployments to the Falklands, managing a three-day overlap in the middle. During our very brief time together there, Bob proposed, and nine weeks after I flew home from the South Atlantic, we were married.

Sadly, just before I returned to the UK, Bob's father, Tom, passed away after a long battle with cancer. I didn't know him well, but he had always been very welcoming and warm, and I have heard many stories about him. I know that he was a proud family man, and Bob felt his loss heavily. His Mum, Irene, must have found our wedding day very tough, being just a few short months after losing Tom, but it was nevertheless a wonderful day, surrounded by family and friends.

Shortly after we married, my time in the RAF was coming to an end, and due to the diverse nature of our work, we knew full well that we would never both be posted to the same place. My options were to either extend my service with the RAF in the knowledge that we'd live apart, or I could leave at this point and we'd be together. It really wasn't a difficult decision - I left, became 'wife of', and my brief but exciting Fighter Control career was over. We bought a house in Elgin, Scotland, near to where Bob was stationed. When I say 'house', I really mean 'project', and we spent the next two years pulling down walls and ceilings, plaster-boarding, fitting bathrooms and kitchen, and only just got the main bits completed before our daughter Rebecca arrived on St Andrews Day in 1992.

All of a sudden I was housewife and mother, and if I'd resembled a rabbit in the headlights before, this was even worse! Whilst I loved being a mum, it can be quite an insular existence, and it began to dawn on me that there's a very good reason why my family were nearly all still living, working and bringing up their children in the place we'd grown up, with their support network very much on the doorstep. Whilst I had been keen to pursue a 'life less ordinary', I now realised that what I had broken away from - and felt I no longer fitted into - was actually something I envied and missed.

Bob spent a lot of Rebecca's early years working away with the RAF. Before he set off back to the Falklands for another six-month stint, he had managed to wangle a move to Cheshire, meaning we could now live in a rented house much nearer to my family, but where we didn't yet know anyone. I was lonely in our new home when he was away. I looked to my sisters for parenting advice and for company, and they were incredibly supportive even though they were still an hour's drive away. I slowly began to finds friends and good neighbours, but I remember my sisters being the ones who helped me through this difficult time.

When Bob returned home, life was good again, and our son Cameron was born in May 1995. Being away so much, Bob had missed far too many of Rebecca's development milestones, which had upset him greatly, and he was keen to be much more a part of Cameron's upbringing. Despite enjoying his RAF career, he decided that enough was enough and took the redundancy package which was being offered to the military at that point, in order to spend more time at home with me and the kids.

We had to quickly think what came next for us, as we were used to a good and regular income, and also because the house we lived in was rented to us through the RAF. Bob had a yearning to be his own boss, and so we looked at buying into a franchise, feeling it might be a safer introduction to the confusing quagmire of running a business. We found a small franchised operation which we quite liked the concept of, and put all our efforts into preparing for this massive step. We'd seen the ideal premises in Carlisle, empty at the time, but which would turn out to be perfect for our new venture. To fund the shop-fit, we spent all of Bob's redundancy money, borrowed the same again, and took out a 100% mortgage on a small house in town. But we set up a 'Delifrance' French-style bakery and café, complete with outside seating area, which at the time was ground-breaking in Carlisle. Looking back, we were a bit reckless to gamble our entire financial future when we had two kids under the age of three, but we had done our homework and planned to work hard – what could go wrong?

Within a short time, we made the business work for us, and quickly established a routine of working alternate day-on, day-off, so that one of us was always at the 'coalface', and the other was at home with the kids. Bob could now spend equal amounts of time working and parenting, definitely making up for lost time as a dad, and I regained a little self-esteem – I was a business owner, and not just a mum. The café was a great success from the outset, and we were soon able to move out of town to a barn conversion with a huge garden in a village just outside Carlisle. The drawbacks were that we rarely got time off together as a family, and as it was a 7-day-a-week operation, we didn't get our weekends together either. On the plus side, we closed at 5pm every day, so we were both around to sit at the table for tea with the kids, and work the bedtime shift together. I have to admit that it was all a culture shock for me - running a business had never been my ambition, and it was a very steep learning curve.

However, after six years of seriously hard work, we decided that we'd had enough, and sold up to the highest bidder. Our financial roulette had paid off, the deal was good for us and we were able to settle the mortgage on our house, with a little left for our next 'project', whatever that would be. Bob was still keen to be his own boss, and we'd learned enough about running a business to be able to risk setting up on our own, rather than through a franchise.

After much thinking, a short course, and weeks of practice, we taught ourselves the art of the chocolatier, and worked hard at turning an idea into a business reality. We started by opening a shop with a viewing window, where customers could watch us working with chocolate, making and piping centres, and hand-rolling truffles, before browsing and hopefully buying. A great idea and quite a glamourous job, but this was also 7-days-a-week, staff reliant, and definitely not a money-spinner. So after around five years we moved away from retail, and into a small production facility which we could now run Monday to Friday, just the two of us. Weekends off at last – but just a shame that the kids were now teenagers, and didn't necessarily want to spend their free time with us! On the flip side, it also meant that we were now spending our whole working, home and leisure time together – no more alternate day-on, day-off, just 24/7 togetherness. Not all relationships would survive this intense cauldron of 'wedded bliss', but we were a good team, each working to our strengths, and we (mostly!) got along fine. It soon became a 'lifestyle' business, earning just enough to manage, but quite an easy and (Christmas aside) fairly stress-free work life.

Alongside running our businesses, a number of huge events had occurred in our personal life. Bob's Mum, Irene, had moved to Cumbria so that she could be nearer to us, and this was lovely. She was at arm's length, but close enough that she could be part of the kids growing up. Unfortunately, soon afterwards she became gripped by Alzheimer's, and although she managed alone for a while, eventually we had to make the heart-breaking decision to move her into a care home, for her own safety. Her flat had to be emptied and sold, which felt wrong when she was still very much alive, and there followed six years of visits to the home to sit with her, even when she no longer knew anyone was there. She was a very proud lady, and it was terribly sad to watch her decline. We scattered her ashes with Tom when she passed away, so they could be together again.

Soon after I first left home for the RAF, Mum and Dad semi and then fully retired to Anglesey in North Wales, where my eldest brother had lived and worked for a number of years. They bought a lovely bungalow in a picturesque village on the coast, and settled in quickly and happily. They made many friends and always seemed to be out with various activity groups, walking, singing, dancing, and of course we all visited regularly for weekends with our own children. Their 12 grandchildren remember very happy times at Granny and Grandad's; fishing, playing on the beach and watching the lifeboat. Mum and Dad were the most patient grandparents – nothing was too much trouble, and they were very generous with their time.

However, as they turned 70, and after 12 contented years there, Dad became worried about their future, as where they lived meant they were completely reliant on him being able to drive. He was keen to sell up and re-locate to somewhere with more on the doorstep, and to start a new life before they were too old to make the move. The flaw in his plan was that their bungalow didn't hold a great value, and they couldn't easily afford anything nice nearer to 'civilisation'. We were still earning well with Delifrance at the time, so we offered to take out a mortgage and buy a place for them which they could rent from us at a manageable rate. They decided on a house a stone's throw from the coast in Morecambe, equidistant from us in Cumbria and the majority of family in Manchester, and they made their move.

With the equity from the bungalow, Bob helped Dad set up several income bonds and savings accounts which were designed to mature or be cashed in at various points over the next 10-12 years, providing a steady income but also leaving easy access to their capital should the need arise. This would have worked a treat if the financial crisis hadn't hit a few years later, seeing interest rates fall dramatically, and Dad cashing in his savings quicker than planned. Without having a crystal ball to see how long they were to need the house (they were now both in their mid-70's), we told a little white lie, assured Dad that we had managed to pay off the mortgage and reduced their rent, which allowed Dad to keep what was left of his savings tucked away. They were back on an even keel, for however long they'd need to be.

They were very happy in their home in Morecambe, immersing themselves into the local community and re-kindling their love of ballroom dancing from years gone by. My siblings and I all visited regularly with our families, and there were many memorable "do's" there. Dad was exceptionally proud of his garden, keeping it looking immaculate all year round, and he had a garage full of woodworking tools which he used often to make us all gifts and keepsakes. One Christmas, we all received our own hand-carved plaque with Dad's favourite word inscribed – Family.

Unfortunately, around this time, Mum was diagnosed with Alzheimer's. Dad straightaway took over all the household responsibilities, but thankfully her condition was a slow-burner, and with his heroic patience, Dad did an amazing job of looking after her on his own.

Growing up in our little rural haven, our daughter, Rebecca, had turned out to be a happy, confident, but very studious girl. She and I had (and still have) a close relationship. Not 'best friends', as I was definitely her nagging mum, but she could confide in me when she wanted to, and we spent a lot of time on our 'girlie dog walks', chatting about life in general. Her future definitely looked promising, and she was determined to get into a good university to study languages. However, a few days after her final GCSE exam (and the day before we were due to fly to Spain for a break), she had a cycling accident as she was on her way to a friends' house to borrow some books for holiday reading. We still don't know what happened, but she was found at the side of the road by a passing ParcelForce delivery driver, and an ambulance was called.

Those first few hours in A & E were a living nightmare. The wonderful NHS staff began their work by assuming the worst-case scenario: spinal injury, brain injury, internal organs. Then by carrying out various tests, scans and x-rays, steadily eliminated possible problems until an accurate diagnosis was made. Bob and I could only watch, hold her hand and try to be upbeat whilst this was going on, but we were deeply shocked as our world unravelled in a blur of white coats. Later that day we were informed that she had 'only' a few injuries, which although not life-threatening, were life-changing. There followed more than three years of operations, treatments and procedures before she was fully discharged. This was an enormous challenge for her to face through her late-teenage years when generally girls are at their most self-conscious. Whilst her friends were spreading their wings, hers were clipped by the fatigue of endless medical appointments and trying to maintain a brave face. There were some very dark days emotionally for her (and us), but she coped admirably well and through sheer determination and hard work, managed to get an amazing set of A level results. She was offered a place at St Andrews University to study French, Spanish and Russian, and loved her five years there, which included time abroad in France and Russia. Her graduation day was a very proud day.

Cameron, on the other hand, was less than studious at school. He was equally bright, although disinterested in academics, but he had a very real talent for music. Like most kids, he'd played the recorder in primary school, which soon led to him learning the flute, and when he arrived at secondary school, he took up the drums. He excelled at all of the above, and scales aside, it was rare that we had to push him to practice, but playing the flute was where his main talent lay. However, whilst we were consumed with helping Rebecca back to strength, we can't have been paying enough attention to Cameron, and at the age of 15 he came off the rails at school. It was more serious than just a bit of bad behaviour, and I blamed myself for not noticing what was before my very eyes, but you don't tend to see things when you're not looking.

We now needed to find time to focus on his needs and to help him get back on the straight and narrow before his mistakes could impact on his future. This coincided with a new music teacher arriving at school, who was young, enthusiastic and fresh out of Music College. Never underestimate the influence that a good teacher can have on an impressionable student… Instead of aiming to study music at a traditional university, she suggested that Cameron should look to conservatoires for his future, as they offered courses which were predominantly performance-based, less academic, and therefore right up his street! However, competition is fierce for those establishments, and he would need extra help, as despite his raw talent and potential, he had to achieve a certain standard to be in with a shout. On his music teacher's advice, he auditioned for, and won, a place in the National Youth Wind Orchestra, and spent a few school holidays living, rehearsing and performing with them. This culminated in a performance at the Royal Albert Hall during the BBC Proms season, one Sunday afternoon in August, and I can't begin to describe the emotion we felt when he walked onto that stage as part of the orchestra. This experience had sparked something inside Cameron too, and from that point he concentrated on his flute studies, to the detriment of his academic subjects, but was rewarded with a scholarship to the Royal Welsh College of Music and Drama in Cardiff. His graduation day too, was a very proud day.

Looking back and taking stock of my life thus far was quite cathartic. For the last 20 years or so I, alongside Bob, had achieved some very good things. We had set-up, run and sold one very successful business, were still running our 'lifestyle' business, and were financially stable. Mum and Dad were becoming older and a little frail, but Dad was still managing as Mum's carer, and whilst we visited and called often, they were not a worry to us. Both our kids had decided on their goals in life and were now aiming directly for them, happy and healthy. So why was I feeling restless? I found that I was longing to find a challenge - something that I could be proud of myself for. Something of my own choosing, something out of the ordinary, and something entirely for my own satisfaction – selfish as it sounds. I guess I was having a mid-life crisis...

My Mid-Life Crisis

Aged 45, and with Cameron in his last A level year at school, I was dreading the whole 'empty nest' that was fast approaching. This happens to a lot of mums, but for me, especially for the last two or three years, my emotional strength had been entirely channelled into trying to support Rebecca through her recovery, and also to encouraging Cameron back onto the right track. I had definitely felt 'needed' and I wasn't looking forward to the imminent change.

I was roped into a fundraising event for the school PTA: a cycle ride coast-to-coast from Tynemouth to Whitehaven, a distance of 183 miles over three days. I was not a cyclist, had barely ridden a bike in the last 15 years, but I relished the challenge, and dusted off the brand new bike we'd bought in case Rebecca ever decided to ride again (she didn't!). For a couple of months, I spent weekends out with a gang of other mums and dads from the school, puffing and pedalling up the hills of the northern Lakes, trying to get in some sort of shape for the looming event. I wasn't particularly fit, was a little overweight, and soon invented a new syndrome I christened 'Cycling Tourette's'. Every time I saw a steep hill appear in the distance, I couldn't help but swear! However, training of sorts completed, the May bank holiday arrived and we set off for Tynemouth to dip our wheels in the sea.

The first day started well, with clear skies, and very little wind. We wended our way inland along the Tyne for a while, and then out into the open Northumbrian countryside. This was bliss - lovely gentle hills, amazing scenery, and great banter with the other riders. It was exciting beyond anything I'd done since RAF days, and as we pottered along the cycle paths and back roads, I felt a wave of happy emotion coursing through me. Frequent refreshment stops gave us a chance to rest a while, eat jelly babies and chocolate, and generally have a laugh, and after lunch, we began to climb up into the hills towards Kielder Forest. That's when the weather started to turn. It wasn't necessarily the increasing drizzle, but the ferocious headwind that was problematic, as we even found we had to pedal to make it downhill. The mood of the riders - and my language - all plummeted, but we made it tired, cold and wet, to our overnight stop at the youth hostel at Kielder, and a few welcome drinks.

The following day was drier, with lighter winds and happier cyclists, and we set off from beautiful Kielder on lovely little lanes and forest tracks, slipping into Scotland before reaching the flatter terrain towards Carlisle. I had studied the route map the previous evening, and saw what can only be described as a monster of a hill, which we were to climb just before we left the forest behind. I was dreading it, so bad it was marked with three chevrons on the map, but I was determined to make it to the top without getting off to push. My legs were only just starting to warm up when there it was - appearing in the distance, strewn with my fellow cyclists, some already pushing, others wobbling and zig-zagging their way up the horrendous incline. I arrived there with my good friend Debbie, and together we swore, shouted and panted upwards, but stayed on two wheels all the way to our 'high five' at the top. I remember thinking that it hadn't been as tough as I'd anticipated, and that's when something sparked inside me. The feeling that I was invincible, and could conquer anything!

The rest of the day was straightforward and without highlight, but finishing just west of Carlisle meant we could all travel home and sleep in our own beds that night. I slept very well indeed, pleased with what I'd done.

The last day was relatively easy, and the sun even shone for the most-part. A 45-mile cruise to the coast, taking in a fair few hills at first, but largely routes I'd practised during training, and then it was mostly downhill after lunch. The refreshment stops were still the best parts of the trip, with lots of banter, camaraderie and pork scratchings, and we could sense the end was in sight. I will never forget cycling along the promenade to the finish point, all of us together, and the overwhelming sense of achievement I felt at having completed such a challenge, coupled with sadness that it was finished. I wanted to cry, to laugh, to sleep, but I also wanted to turn round and do it all over again. We were met at the finish line by friends and family, and even one of my sisters had driven up from Manchester to witness our arrival at the coast. Priceless.

We all got together that evening to share stories, beers and fish & chips, and I remember someone jokingly saying "So, is it Land's End to John O'Groats next then Jane?!". And there it was – the seed had been planted. The seed that niggled and grew. The seed that was there when I woke up, and chipped away at me all day long. I began to secretly research the journey online, and the further I looked into it, the more my desire was fuelled. I was excited by the idea of doing something on my own, completely out of character, and something that was such a serious challenge. I didn't have the confidence to attempt it unsupported, and I knew that Bob would never be able to follow me in the car, as one of us would need to run the chocolate business. So I would have to buy into a fully supported trip, which would come at a price. There are companies out there who organise supported charity runs, but they seemed to travel the distance in too short a time for me and I would never keep up. Other companies arrange the trip on a budget, and you have to pitch your tent each evening, but the thought of sleeping under canvas after a long day in the saddle definitely didn't appeal.

However, I found one company - Peak Tours - who run fully supported cycling 'holidays', and Land's End to John O'Groats was one of them. With this company, it would take 14 days of cycling an average of 75 miles a day, but it looked like an amazing trip, and I really, really fancied the challenge. I honestly can't remember how I finally broached the subject with Bob, but I do know that he was surprised, but happy for me to have a go. By the September, I was booked onto a trip for the following May with Peak Tours, feeling guilty about the cost, and the time away from the business which it would require, but it was incredibly exciting, and after all, I felt I deserved it.

And so it began – the epic challenge which was my official mid-life crisis!

Land's End to John O'Groats (LeJog)

Having bought a proper road bike to replace the cheap hybrid I'd been riding, I had to put it all to the back of my mind for the autumn. September to December in the life of a chocolatier doesn't leave much time for anything other than Christmas chocolates, and we were too busy even to feel the 'empty nest' now that Cameron had just left for Cardiff. When the New Year arrived, I began to plan ahead and get prepared for the trip. I spent January and February getting fitter, popping out on my bike when the weather wasn't too bad, and planning my training regime. Peak Tours sent a suggested 10-week training programme, aimed at transforming a reasonably fit casual cyclist into someone able to take on the challenge of LeJog. I amended the programme a little to increase the length of some of the rides, in the knowledge that I was probably less able a cyclist than most who would be daft enough to take on this venture. But by the end of February I began my official training schedule, and stuck to it avidly.

Most of my rides would be at weekends, and as this was traditionally a quiet time for chocolatiers, I could arrange most Fridays off as well. I had been advised that consecutive days in the saddle were better preparation than spreading rides out over the week, so that's what I tried to do. As the lighter evenings approached, I was able to escape work early some days, leaving Bob to clean up and finish off whilst I put in the miles. I was getting fitter, never missed a training run, did most of these rides alone, but was loving every single minute of it. Even the hills (of which there were many around where we lived) didn't faze me anymore – I just dropped into low gear, took in the view, and I'd crawled up to the top before I'd even had chance to swear! I had wanted to be fit enough to be able to enjoy the cycling, absorb the scenery, and make the most of every day of the trip – time would tell if I'd achieved that.

So this was it: 12 months of planning, four months and 1664 miles of training, two tubs of nappy cream finished, and I was about to jump on a train towards Land's End. I wasn't nervous, just really excited - I felt a freedom which is difficult to describe, and the fact that I was travelling on my own was very much a part of the adventure. As the countryside rolled past the carriage windows, I was amazed to think that the following day would see me re-trace this journey by pedal-power – it seemed a hell of a long way! Three trains later, and I was pulling into Penzance, to be met by the Peak Tours support crew, who took me to the Youth Hostel at St Just to settle in. That evening, my fellow cyclists and I met up for dinner at a local pub, had our 'welcome' briefing, and began to get acquainted. There were some small groups who were clearly doing this together, at least one husband and wife team, and a couple of sisters from Scotland, but there were also a handful of us 'solo' adventurers. So far, so good, but nerves were beginning to set in now...

Day 1. Land's End to Fowey
Miles – 64
Ascent – 4500ft

We awoke to lovely sunshine, accompanied by strong winds, and we had six miles to cycle to the start point at Land's End. It was immediately clear to me that most of the others were indeed pretty good cyclists, who could hold a conversation on the steep hills, barely pausing for breath! Oh well, I'd be happy bringing up the rear... At the south-westerly tip of mainland UK, we had the obligatory photo-call by the sign, and a safety briefing from Peak Tours - ironically whilst standing in front of a wall covered in plaques commemorating all those who have died attempting this challenge. And then we were off!

I stayed towards the back of the pack on the pretence of needing to get used to using the satnav I'd hired with the route loaded, but I know I'd have found myself at the rear pretty quickly anyway. I'd heard that the first three days are considered the hardest of the trip, as the terrain in Devon and Cornwall is renowned for its steep, rugged beauty. I was determined to pedal every inch of the way without getting off to push, but I failed in the first 15 miles! In my defence, this was on a stretch of flat promenade at Penzance, which was six inches deep in soft sand following the recent storms – surely that doesn't count? The hills were frighteningly steep but thankfully short, and there were plenty of them, but I managed to keep my head up to take in the scenery. I was joined at the back by a few others as the day went on, and we pedalled and chatted in between panting up the hills. I felt exhilarated and incredibly fortunate to be on my bike, cycling through parts of the UK that I had only seen in pictures. This was definitely the life, and I was still smiling as I went to bed that night.

Day 2. Fowey to Moretonhampstead
Miles – 61
Ascent – 4500ft

This was the day that felt much tougher than the above figures show. Some seriously steep short hills in the morning along the coastline to Plymouth, followed by a mammoth steady climb up onto Dartmoor. The scenery in the morning was stunning – lovely sandy coves and dramatic cliffs, which we mostly saw from quiet back lanes. It was still quite windy, and as we passed through Plymouth, we had a heavy rain shower with a smattering of hail. I had been riding with a small pack of mostly solo cyclists, but as we approached Dartmoor after lunch, the horizontal drizzle set in, and we all spread out to crawl up onto the plateau at our own pace. Had the mist lifted, it would have been a lovely view! I vividly remember the feeling of icy cold drizzle running into my right ear, and dripping down under my collar, steadily soaking me through.

It felt lonely through this last section of the day, and I was a little apprehensive about what was to come for the rest of the trip. However, I arrived at my B&B, to be met by the lovely landlord, who offered to wash and dry my soaked clothes. What a lovely man he was, but he DID like to chat, and I had a date with a hot shower. Finally, I made my excuses and found my room, and boy was it good to take off my sodden shoes! I had to get off to push twice today – once on an enforced detour around some storm repairs in Looe which sent us up a very steep footpath which wasn't really fit for cycling, and then on a very short but monstrous climb out of Plymouth. Had the first incident been on tarmac, it might have been different, but no excuses for the second one – my legs just couldn't take it! Maybe I'd manage the whole of the next day on two wheels...?

Day 3. Moretonhampstead to Glastonbury
Miles – 72
Ascent – 4000ft

Day three was simply spectacular. The weather was dry, bright and warm, and would remain so for the next few days. There were some long slow hills early on as we were leaving Dartmoor but it was beautiful countryside, and I passed carpets of bluebells, thatched cottages, and views for miles. This felt like cycling at its best, and I couldn't have been happier. We picked our way across the Exeter conurbation, followed by a relatively flat section before lunch. I rode these last few miles with Pat, a fellow solo traveller, and we both confided that we were bitterly disappointed at having to push up 'heartbreak hill' the day before. We knew from the route map that there was a serious ascent straight after lunch, so when we got there, the pair of us stuck together, battling upwards to the top. He obviously found it much easier than I did, but he stayed with me, cheering me on, and we were quite rightly proud of ourselves at the top. Turns out, I wouldn't need to get off and push up a hill ever again on this trip!

The last few miles were mostly on farm tracks and very quiet lanes through the Somerset Levels, and thankfully, they live up to their name. In the distance we could see our destination, Glastonbury Tor towering over the landscape. But it had been a special day, and an evening in Glastonbury was the icing on the cake, as it's a place which has to be experienced to be believed.

Day 4. Glastonbury to Monmouth
Miles – 64
Ascent – 2900ft

I knew there were some iconic tourist sights en-route today, and I wanted to make sure I saw them all. It was a gloriously sunny day, and after a few short miles we arrived in the tiny but bustling city of Wells. With a few others I stopped off to take photos, have a wander around the farmers market, and soak up the atmosphere of this magical place with its cathedral and ancient buildings steeped in history. I made a mental note to come back here with Bob sometime, as it was the most beautiful city, and I knew he'd love it. Little did I know that some years later, Cameron would live and work here, so we've now been plenty of times, and it's still one of my favourite places to visit.

Leaving Wells, there was a most enormous hill to ascend along the Old Bristol Road, but I was getting fitter every day, and although my Cycling Tourette's made a brief but loud appearance, I managed to stay on two wheels, albeit with shaky legs! We entered Bristol via a lovely country park, with stunning views all across the city, before we crossed the

Clifton Suspension Bridge over the dramatic gorge below. This really was the life – sunshine, very little wind, and some of the best sights the UK can offer. North from Bristol we crossed the river Severn over the old crossing, and on to Chepstow, where the punters were out in their finery, staggering back to the car park after a day at the races. Leaving Chepstow came one of the best stretches of road of the whole trip. A lovely long descent to the haunting Tintern Abbey, and onwards beside the meandering river Wye all the way to Monmouth: beautiful scenery, smooth tarmac, gentle descent and a massive smile. I didn't want this day to end.

Day 5. Monmouth to Clun
Miles – 58
Ascent – 3300ft

Today was billed as the shortest day of the trip, and one of the flattest. I had been pretty much the last one to arrive at the finish point each evening, but I had now been joined at the rear by four others, two pairs of friends. Although we all set off with the main pack in the morning, by the first brew-stop, the five of us found ourselves riding as a group at a very similar pace, and really enjoying each other's company. At 58 miles, I was looking forward to an easy day in the saddle – my legs were beginning to tire, and I needed to complete some domestic chores. Anyway, it would just be lovely to have a proper rest before going out for dinner, and maybe, just maybe, I might not need such an early night tonight...

There was a big hill straight out of Monmouth, but after that the route was described as 'undulating'. My legs felt like it was a bit more challenging than that, but after the first hill, we wended our way through some lovely 'black and white' villages, with thatch and Tudor definitely the order of the day. We passed through Hereford, entering via a lovely traffic-free cycle path following an old railway line, and leaving on some pretty busy main roads. But then we were back onto the lovely quiet country lanes heading for our night stop at Clun in Shropshire.

This winter had seen some severe storms, with much flooding and wind damage throughout the UK. We had seen evidence of the damage, and been detoured by the repair works several times so far, and today was no different. About 12 miles from Clun, the road was closed and unusually, the workmen were not letting cyclists or pedestrians through. The detour would add more than 20 miles to our day, or there was a three mile footpath through woodland nearby, bringing us back to the route. Some set off for the big detour, but the majority opted for the woodland, including me and my fellow 'rear gunners'. I knew it was a mistake as soon as we committed, but we pressed on up an incredibly muddy footpath, which no-one could cycle through on a road bike. Pushing and walking, slipping and sliding, it was funny at first, but after a mile or so, it was torture. The second mile was a little drier and flatter, but still definitely mountain bike terrain, and we realised our early finish was not to be. By now we were caked in mud up to the knees, our bikes heavily clogged, and our tempers long since frayed.

When we eventually reached tarmac, it was a miserable few miles pedalling and dripping mud to Clun, where I just couldn't help the tears welling up, thinking of how much I had wanted an early and easy finish to the day. Instead, I was shattered, filthy, and only just in time for dinner – if I got a rush on! Thankfully, the tears attracted the attention of one of our tour guides, and he soon had me and my bike hosed down. No domestic chores done, no rest before dinner, but a nice shiny clean bike....

Day 6. Clun to Runcorn
Miles – 79
Ascent – 2400ft

After such an eventful day yesterday, today was meant to be pretty flat, although a long day in the saddle, and we were blessed with another beautiful day. There were a couple of hills early on, but even I would describe today as 'undulating'. We passed some incredibly beautiful countryside, through the lovely town of Shrewsbury, and pressed almost directly north over the flat Shropshire and Cheshire plains towards Runcorn. The road surfaces had been poor yesterday and for most of today, which was playing havoc with my backside and wrists, but the miles were rushing by on the flat roads, so it was all worth it. Although the scenery was stunning at times, there were also long stretches with high hedges, and so I would say that this was the most boring of all the days riding, if I really had to choose!

The last 10 miles or so were on much busier roads, and it was late afternoon on a Friday, with the traffic building. We stayed in small groups, naturally the five of us 'slowies' at the back together, and just pushed on to our final destination – the Holiday Inn at Runcorn. Up to now, we'd been in some quaint and quirky accommodation. Mostly privately owned B&B's, and occasionally Youth Hostels, but they had all been clean, comfy, and with friendly and helpful welcomes. This was different. Anonymous boxes for rooms, loud and expensive bar and restaurant, but a pool if you had enough energy for a swim – I didn't! However, on the plus side, the Wi-Fi was incredibly fast, and I spent much of the evening after dinner catching up on emails and writing my blog.

Day 7. Runcorn to Garstang
Miles – 65
Ascent – 3300ft

Today started flat, but this was the most 'urban' section of the route so far. Whilst we'd been through some big towns and busy cities already, they had largely been geared up for cyclists, but today we had to skirt around some major conurbations such as Warrington, Bolton and Blackburn, and the roads on our route were shared with drivers good and bad. You have to concentrate a lot more through the towns, not only on staying safe, but on navigation, as you really don't want to veer off route in the confusion of busy streets. But just before lunch, we thankfully headed out of Bolton, and up onto the quiet Lancashire moors. There was quite a climb at first, but at least we were in the freshest of air, and the reward was a lovely descent with stunning views of reservoirs and sailing boats.

After lunch at a typically Lancashire 'local', we picked our way around Blackburn, and onwards north towards our stop at Garstang, passing rolling hills and bright green heather. Today had been hot – very hot - although the sunshine made sure we were all still smiling as we drifted to the hotel. I have to confess that by this time, my legs were tiring towards the end of each day, but I was very much looking forward to the next two days, and being close to home.

Day 8. Garstang to Keswick
Miles – 65
Ascent – 4000ft

Today was to be a special day for me, as I would be passing near to Mum and Dad's house in Morecambe, onwards through familiar territory, finishing near home, and I was especially excited to be spending a night in my own bed - with Bob. Mum and Dad had wanted to follow me along part of the route today, but Dad had car trouble. Bob had offered to drive down to them early morning, pick them up, and meet us at the first brew-stop so they could cheer me on. I know Mum and Dad were incredibly proud of what I was doing, and following my daily blog avidly, so to pass close by their home and not have the chance for them meet the other cyclists I'd been writing about, would have been a shame.

We left Garstang and followed a lovely cycle path along the coastline and around the edge of Lancaster, from where we travelled north through Carnforth and into the Lancashire countryside proper. I kept my eye out for Bob, Mum and Dad, and sure enough, there they all were at the first stop. It was really good to see them, and have them meet the 'team', especially the four lads whose company I was keeping each day at the back of the pack. But I couldn't hang around too long if I wanted to finish at a reasonable hour, so Bob took

Mum and Dad home, intending to meet me again at the lunch stop in Kendal. However, he was to get stuck in an enormous traffic jam following an accident on the motorway, so he didn't catch up with me again until late afternoon.

In the meantime, we cycled through some of the most breath-taking scenery that the UK has to offer, passing most of the main tourist sights of the Lake District. The incentive of getting home made me feel invincible today. My speed increased, my legs didn't tire, and my smile was enormous as I blasted past Windermere, Ambleside, Grasmere, Rydal, without even stopping to take photos. This was my home turf, and I could come back for pictures any time! At the afternoon brew-stop, Bob had been freed from the M6 carpark, and had his bike in the back of the car. We pedalled happily together along the length of Thirlmere, before he turned back to pick up the car and I plodded on up the hills to Keswick, where we were to finish for the day. A spectacular days cycling, and an even better welcome at home! Bob cooked Chateaubriand for the two of us, and I sipped Pinot Grigio in the garden whilst the washing machine was working full pelt, and Bob gave my bike some TLC. I even managed a Skype chat with both kids (Rebecca was studying in Russia at the time), and of course I got my fix of cuddles from the dogs too. I could quite happily have had a day off, re-charging the batteries, but no rest for the wicked...

Day 9. Keswick to Moffat
Miles – 74
Ascent - 4000ft

After a wonderful night's sleep, Bob reluctantly loaded me into the car, and we headed back to the start-line at Keswick to meet my fellow cyclists. There were some nasty hills this morning, but it was all along routes I'd cycled many times during training. I was able to warn the others of the potholes and pitfalls, but also tell them where to stop to take in the best views. The morning brew-stop was less than two miles from home, at the top of a long slow hill. From a distance, I could see a good few cars and spectators by the brew van – friends of ours who were there to cheer me on. Our neighbour had even placed handwritten signs of encouragement along the route here, one pointing out the 'last big hill in England', which we all gathered around for a team photo! A few of our friends had brought their bikes, and cycled along with me to the lunch stop at Gretna. It was just lovely to have familiar company, and to know that people were following my progress – it made it all seem worthwhile! Bob again met us at the lunch stop, but as we crossed into Scotland, we said our farewells for another week, and I re-joined my four teammates bringing up the rear.

Passing the sign 'Welcome to Scotland' was a milestone for us all – just one country to go now! For the southerners in the group, passing into Scotland seemed to be near the finish line, but there were still five and a half long days of cycling left before we reached the very top. Several of the group were caught in a cloudburst early on which soaked them through (us tail-end Charlies managed to miss it), and there were a number of punctures on the significant potholes which seemed to be the norm in this part of Scotland. I fared well, but the last few miles towards Moffat were along a strength-sapping incline, and after the exhilaration of the last two days, my legs suddenly felt like lead again.

Day 10. Moffat to Balloch
Miles – 81
Ascent – 2900ft

I woke refreshed, and we set off up a long, slow climb out of Moffat. The scenery was so very beautiful, that I quite forgot the hill, and just enjoyed the view as I plodded steadily upwards. I was back to really enjoying riding, and so didn't stop to take pictures, just absorbed the panorama, the air and the quiet roads. After the first climb, we popped out at the top of a hill overlooking the M74 motorway, which runs parallel to the Carlisle-Glasgow railway line, and follows the path of Evan Water – a tributary of the River Annan. It's a stunning sight, looking down on the running water, cars and trains, and the next few miles were on a B-road which criss-crossed all three, and was obviously once the only route through here. The road surface was appalling now. Not potholes as such, just really rough and in dire need of repair. However, I suppose the motorway takes precedence, and I strongly suspect that this road surface will remain as bad for years.

Lunch was just south of Glasgow at Chatelherault – built as a folly and hunting lodge, it is now a country park and visitor centre with amazing views over the city. That was the end of the climbing for the day, and after a short section of very busy roads, we joined a lovely cycle path along the banks of the River Clyde. It was quiet, with a good surface, mercifully flat, and before we knew it we were in the heart of Glasgow. I hadn't anticipated such a lovely arrival in the city, and was blown away by the beauty of this part of the centre. We very quickly joined a canal towpath, which led us on to a cycleway along the banks of the River Leven, which eventually brought us out at the southern end of Loch Lomond in the town of Balloch. This had been a real eye-opener for me. Since lunch, we had been almost entirely traffic-free, on purpose-built cycle routes, and enjoying gorgeous scenery. I had never imagined that such a huge city, with a reputation like Glasgow's, could offer such amazing cycling.

Day 11. Balloch to Glencoe
Miles – 67
Ascent – 3100ft

Today began with another lovely cycle path, this time alongside Loch Lomond. The banks are indeed 'bonny', and there was lots of stopping for photos, and just taking in the lakeside views. At the northern end of the loch - the touristy part - we had to join the main A82 and stay with it for much of the day. This is a busy road, narrow in places, and the chances for cars to overtake in between the twisty turns were few and far between. After being on the flat yesterday afternoon and this morning, the hills came as a shock to the system, as did the lorries and coaches which frequent this road. But we pressed on in small groups, trying not to anger the motorists who were going about their business, through Crianlarich and Tyndrum, and into the Highlands. Here, the landscape opened up and, having had our heads down for much of the last few miles, we were greeted by spectacular countryside.

However, the weather was changing rapidly, and although sunny, we were now riding against a building headwind. Dropping down into the valley nearing Glencoe, we were fighting against the wind which slowed us to a crawl, but it didn't stop us from admiring the majesty of our surroundings. We made it to our end point for the day, tired and cold, but excited at the scenery we had ridden past and the thought of similar to come. There were a few riders who had never been this far north before, and I spent a quiet five minutes at the afternoon brew-stop with one bloke who had just found the true meaning of the word 'breath-taking'. The moisture in his eyes as he stood in silence just staring out over his cuppa at the mountains, was quite moving. Our accommodation that night was in a youth hostel, in woodland, by a river. Sounds picturesque? Well, it would have been if it hadn't been for the midges! Our vision of sitting out after dinner with a beer or two was scuppered by the ferocious bugs, and despite sleeping with all the windows closed, I still managed to wake up with bites on anything that had been sticking out from under the covers...

Day 12. Glencoe to Inverness
Miles – 82
Ascent – 4400ft

For me, today was to prove the hardest of the whole trip. The mileage was long, and although the hills were mostly towards the end of the day, they were significant climbs. But the worst part was the wind – ferocious headwinds, rattling through the valleys as though through a wind tunnel, hampering our progress all day. I think the problem started before we left the youth hostel. It is usually a bring-your-own affair there, but Peak Tours had arranged for us cyclists to have breakfast provided. It was self-serve, but there wasn't much of a spread, and so I ended up with just a banana and a slice of toast, mindful to leave some of the rations for the others. Normally that would suffice, but at the start of an 82 mile slog, I needed more fuel, and tiredness set in quickly.

We set off as our usual team of five at the back, and headed along the A82 to Fort William, dodging the lorries, and taking turns to be the windbreak at the front. Fort William would have been lovely if I could've seen it all, but there was low cloud, mist, and my mind was on reaching the next brew-stop to take on calories. From there, we made our way up a long but gentle route paralleling the Caledonian Canal, overlooking the odd ship below. I'd love to go back and cycle this road in good weather, as I feel cheated that I missed some spectacular views, and my memory of it is tainted by the fatigue. When we finally arrived at the brew van at the commando memorial at Spean Bridge, we should have been staring at the might of Ben Nevis, but instead we just layered up against the swirling mist, drank hot drinks and ate plenty. Then, we had to take another stretch of the infamous A82 to Fort Augustus for lunch, where it had started raining, and looked unlikely to stop for the rest of the day.

Lunch was followed by an enormous climb out of town, taking us to the military road which runs on the east side of

Loch Ness – a much quieter road, but a very serious ascent. I had put on my waterproof jacket and some long trousers, as it was getting cold as well as wet, but this meant that I began to overheat on the monstrous hill. It took me well over an hour to reach the top, by which time the rain had turned to sleet, and despite my extra layers I got very cold on the descent to the brew van. There was only 20 miles of 'undulations' left to pedal, but the inclines felt like mountains, and my legs felt like lead weights. I was cold, wet, tired, and my bottom lip had started to wobble. I knew I was slowing down the rest of our group, so made them press on to get warm, and for the first time on the trip I was riding alone, but with the Peak Tours guide cycling just behind me at the back. He could see I was struggling, but held back so as not to patronise me with false words of encouragement. This was *my* challenge, and I just had to get on and deal with it. Eventually, Inverness loomed on the horizon, and I slipped into my hotel room, to spend far too long in the shower, a take-away pizza and a very early night.

Day 13. Inverness to Altnaharra
Miles – 73
Ascent - 3300ft

I woke in much better spirits, refreshed and determined not to let the elements defeat me today. We left Inverness in biting cold wind, but the hills soon warmed us, and we followed cycle paths and quiet roads to Dingwall and on to Bonar Bridge. There were some stunning views, oil rigs being built in the estuary, and the threatening clouds made everything look atmospheric. Our lunch stop was at a pub where we could get warm, eat well, and put on more layers as required. It was forecast to rain this afternoon, and the sky certainly looked as though it would keep its promise.

When we arrived in Lairg late afternoon, there was just one gradual gradient left to conquer before our finish point, but it was a long climb. Normally, this wouldn't have been a problem as it was a very gentle incline, but it was a good 15 miles or so up exposed rolling moorland, with absolutely no shelter from the headwind. The road was single-track with passing places and frequent, wet cattle grids. Although we felt like we were in the middle of nowhere, the route was surprisingly busy, but I wasn't pulling in and stopping for anyone – I just kept my head down, slogging upwards until The Crask Inn came into sight. This is a very old coaching inn, and clearly the only refuge for miles around. Some of our group were staying there, others were being ferried back to accommodation in Lairg, but me and my four fellow tail-enders were to press on a little further to a B&B at Altnaharra. We didn't relish the thought of an extra seven miles today, but it meant that we had a head start on the others in the morning for the last day. Peak Tours clearly hoped that this would mean we had a chance of reaching the finish point (John O'Groats) all together, and not too spread out. We had the best night! Our wonderful landlady washed and dried all of our wet stuff, made us an amazing home-cooked stew and syrup sponge, and a hearty breakfast, before we headed off for our final day's ride.

Day 14. Altnaharra to John O'Groats
Miles – 75

Ascent – 3700ft

Boy, was I looking forward to today! The five of us set off earlier than usual, mindful that an early start meant an early finish, and we were already seven miles ahead of the speedy peloton. Today was dull and grey, but not a breath of wind, and so we really enjoyed laughing and chatting along the peaceful road out of Altnaharra, meandering alongside the River Naver slowly downhill to the first brew-stop. We arrived before the brew van did – definitely a first for our group! We pressed on towards lunch, but as we left the riverside behind, there was quite a climb to Bettyhill, and our first glimpse of the North Sea. It was a spectacular and very welcome sight: golden sand with vivid blue waves crashing in and spray blowing over the sand dunes.

But it's here that a funny thing happened. Your mind works in mysterious ways, and having seen the coastline, and knowing that I'd cycled coast-to-coast already, my brain decided to tell my legs that they'd done enough. Goal achieved, time to relax and rest. It was a bit like the marathon runners who collapse with the finish line in sight, except I still had 40 miles to cover to my finish line, and it certainly wasn't all flat!

By lunchtime, we had been caught and passed by most of the others, but they were cruising now, and I was definitely struggling. Through gritted teeth and with shaky legs I kept going, watching the cliffs of the coastline roll by on my left, fields and farms on my right, and the rest of our group disappearing in the distance. I was the last to make it to the village of Mey, and a pub where everyone else was waiting to re-group and cycle the last few miles to the finish together. Despite my fatigue, it was a wonderful feeling - all cycling together, singing and laughing, heading for the place we'd aimed for over the last 14 days.

When we finally arrived, there was a glass of fizz awaiting, a few tears, and the obligatory photo shoot, but I spent a few minutes alone, just looking out to sea, feeling elated, and a little overwhelmed. I had pedalled from one end of the country to the other, covered almost 1000 miles, spent 94 hrs 53 mins in the saddle, and climbed more than one and a half times the height of Everest. Wow!

Now I could be officially proud of myself! Years later, I still glow when I see the weather map on TV, and imagine the line between Land's End and John O'Groats. It's one hell of a distance, and such an amazing achievement. I took in all of my surroundings every day, and can still picture almost every inch of the journey. It had been such a special experience, and I longed to do it all over again – once I'd had a damned good sleep! Straightaway, I vowed that for my 50th, I would again enrol with Peak Tours, and this time cycle from coast to coast through France, from the Channel to the Med. A slightly shorter distance, at 880 miles, with equally, if not more challenging ascents, but this 'End-to-End' had certainly inspired me to aim for another adventure. I was only just approaching 47, and so had plenty of time to plan and get ready for it.

Total Miles - 980
Total Ascent - 50,300ft

For anyone interested in statistics, the above ascent figures were an approximation based on my original route notes. For the trip through France, the ascent figures are taken from a Garmin satnav, and although they're more reliable, they're still not 100% accurate.

Peak Tours have since changed their route for LeJog, and they no longer follow the Great Glen or spend time on the infamous A82.

My 50ᵗʰ Year

After LeJog I felt elated, and vowed that I would be out on my bike at every opportunity, but first I had some family time to catch up on, lots of tales to tell in our local pub, and some well-earned R&R. This R&R seemed to extend beyond a couple of months, and my big plans to keep up with my cycling soon took a back seat. There was still a business to run, family to keep on top of, Pinot Grigio to drink, and I found that I seemed to develop the knack of finding a good excuse as to why I couldn't get out on my bike that day…. or the next. The menopause hit, I gained weight and apathy, and my bike grew cobwebs in the garage. But that's OK, I told myself, I still have my goal of cycling through France for my 50ᵗʰ. I'd trained from scratch once before, and I could do it a second time, couldn't I?

So, as my 49ᵗʰ birthday peered over the horizon, I intended to mark the occasion by booking my place on the Peak Tours Channel to the Med trip for a date around my 50ᵗʰ. After all, once it was booked there could be no excuses to be lazy – I would simply HAVE to get out on my bike again, and I knew that once I got started, my cycling mojo would come flooding back.

Around this time, we'd become very proficient at running the chocolate business in pretty much three long days a week, and Bob and I found that we had much more free time to ourselves. We'd done lots of fell walking, spent some weekends away, and had generally been soul-searching about our future. I loved our house in Cumbria. It wasn't pretty, but it was practical, and with a massive garden. It had been perfect for our growing kids and a steady stream of rescue dogs, but now there was just the two of us, and it was starting to feel like time to downsize. This was where we had to make our big decision. Should we sell the house and buy something smaller locally, or should we have a complete change and move to pastures new?

Rebecca had by now moved into a flat in Cheshire with her boyfriend James, and was teaching French and Spanish in a school in Warrington. She and James were very happy together, he was successfully climbing the ladder professionally, and we felt very comfortable that he seemed to be 'the one'. It was unlikely that they would move back to Cumbria anytime soon. Cameron had just accepted a job at Wells Cathedral School, and was going to live there on the school premises. His future was a little more uncertain, but we were confident that Cumbria wouldn't be his pick of places to try to earn a living as a classical musician. So we came to the conclusion that, friends aside, there was nothing to keep us 'up north'.

If we were to move away, what should we do with the business? Take it with us? Sell it? Relocating would mean lots of hard work, as we would have to find suitable premises and a whole new customer base - you can't supply 'local' chocolates from hundreds of miles away. We didn't relish the thought of effectively starting anew. But to sell felt awkward – the business was *us*, with our skills and our back-story; new owners would need to quickly learn what took us months, if not years, to master. So, slowly but surely, we came to the life-changing decision that we should advertise the house, and if it sold we'd simply close down the business, move to a completely different area, and then decide what comes next. But let's not get too carried away – we had to sell the house first, and that might not be straightforward.

As is often the case, one big decision leads to another, and I knew that I should postpone my plans for my French bike ride. Before we could put the house on the market, we needed to spend a bit of time and money on freshening it up. And on the off-chance that it did sell quickly, we'd need to have some sort of plan as to where we would look to buy our new home. That wouldn't leave much time for me to get fit and put in the miles required for training. So, instead of planning to complete my ride around my 50th, I set a new goal of riding 'in the year I turned 50', and didn't book the trip.

In the early summer, a bizarre chain of events took place, which assured us that this move was meant to be, and didn't leave us with much time to dither over decisions. The catalyst was the house sale. Having done a little decorating inside and out, we were ready to invite in the estate agents. However, in the dark recesses of my brain, I remembered a chance comment at a wine tasting event some months before, during a conversation with a girl who used to work for us as a student. She was now very successful, married and with two young boys. She had asked if we still lived in 'that lovely big house', and had said that it was just the kind of place she and her husband would love to bring up their children. I got in touch with her to tell her we had decided to sell, they came to view, and loved it as much as we did! As we weren't in a rush, and as they now needed to try to sell their own home, we agreed to re-convene in three months' time. However, theirs sold a fortnight later and we now had to decide, and quickly, where we wanted to live...

During the course of the last two years, we'd spent a number of weekends away, visiting towns and cities on our 'possible places' list. Amongst others, these included Worcester, Malvern, Hereford and Shrewsbury. We had a wish list consisting of:

* A bit of 'culture' within easy driving distance.
* A good pub within walking distance.
* Public transport to the nearest big town.
* A shop for the basics within walking distance.
* Good transport links, so we could visit family easily.
* Did I mention a good pub within walking distance?

Shrewsbury currently topped our list, and when we were last there we had visited a small development of new-builds in a village about 10 miles north of town, which ticked all of our boxes and more. But that had been months ago, and surely all those houses would now be sold? Well, apparently not! There were just 2 properties still available in our price bracket, so we drove down, reassured ourselves that this was a place we thought we could live, and placed a deposit.

Now we had to wind down the business, sell off the equipment and assets, but we wanted to give our retail customers as much notice as we could, to allow them time to find a new chocolate supplier. As soon as we announced our plans to close, a local couple expressed an interest in purchasing the business as a going concern. We hadn't thought seriously about selling, but now that time was pressing, it seemed much more appealing than trying to find buyers for the mountain of equipment we'd accumulated. We quickly needed to work out some form of training course, and to set the wheels in motion to transfer the lease on our production unit. But we came up with a plan, and four weeks later we handed over the keys, following a whirlwind masterclass in how our business worked, and how to make delicious chocolates. It was quite sad after 14 years of building our brand to simply walk away, but it felt like the right decision for us.

My 50th birthday happened to fall exactly one week before we were to leave our home of 21 years, and begin our new chapter in Shropshire. We celebrated at our local pub, with Rebecca and James, Cameron, and a few of our closest friends – an emotional but happy evening, from what I can remember… What I DO remember clearly is that my good friend Debbie (from the first coast-to-coast ride) drunkenly vowed to do the French trip with me, which promised to be a great partnership. I could now look forward to sharing this amazing experience, to having a room-mate to banter with, and a soulmate to swear up the hills with. We soon booked our trip for the following May - still within the year I turned 50!

The house move went as smoothly as these things can, and we began to settle into our new home and explore our new surroundings. Our big 'plan' was to get comfortable throughout the autumn, then enjoy Christmas and New Year, before I began to train again in earnest to be ready for the trip in May. Once the bike ride was over, I'd start to look for work. I had decided I'd had enough of being self-employed, and fancied the idea of working for someone else part-time, but until then I was calling this my 'gap year'. Bob would perhaps look into another small enterprise, or maybe even into volunteer work - but first, we had friends to make, neighbours to get to know, and a whole new county to discover.

We started our search for friends at the local pub....

The Bombshell

Having moved just six weeks before, we couldn't be happier! We were getting used to the down-size, the neighbours seemed great, and the local countryside was filled with walking trails and canal networks. We spent our days in the fresh air of an Indian summer, and our evenings either in the garden or in the pub – well, you have to make the effort to fit in with the locals…

But then came the phone call that would change everything for me.

Mum had fallen at home, and Dad was following the ambulance to the hospital in Lancaster. My two sisters were on their way there, so there was no point in me jumping in the car until they arrived and evaluated the situation.

Before I move on, it would be opportune to outline my immediate family tree, to make the next chapter easier to understand. In age order….

Mum and Dad – now both aged 88 and still living in the house we bought in Morecambe. Mum's Alzheimer's aside, they were both in good health, although Dad recently had a few problems with his 'waterworks'. He was still Mum's sole carer and managing fine.

Anne – lives in Manchester, recently retired.

Rick – lives on Anglesey, works full-time as a company director.

John – lives in Manchester, took over Dad's plumbing business, and so works for himself.

Sue – lives in Manchester, works full-time, and was recently ordained as a vicar.

Me – now living in Shropshire, not currently working.

Whilst we were a fairly close family, we didn't spend lots of time with each other. When we did get together, we had the best of times, but we could go months or even years in between family "do's". I probably caught up with my sisters by phone most months, but only really Christmas and birthdays with my brothers. But at times like these, family comes first, and we all immediately rallied round.

Anne and Sue made it to the hospital in time to see Mum before she went into surgery. She had broken a hip and needed a replacement joint. Dad was obviously in shock, and probably very grateful the cavalry had arrived. By the time the initial firefighting was over, they reported back to the rest of us that Mum would be in hospital for at least a couple of weeks until she was back on her feet properly. Dad was very tired, and in a bit of a tizz about how Mum would cope without him there all the time, as she wouldn't understand what was happening or where she was. It was clear that he needed our help, so we set up a rota to stay with him so he wouldn't have to drive himself to visit Mum when his mind was elsewhere, and so that he didn't neglect his own needs. It would only be a couple of weeks, so it wouldn't be a problem…

As is often the case (we're reliably informed), Mum woke the next day in complete confusion. The fall, the anaesthetic, the drugs, the strange surroundings, had all contributed to her Alzheimer's taking a nosedive, although she still knew us. The doctors said there was a chance that she'd be back to herself in a few days, but that often this sudden decline would be permanent. Dad was deeply distressed by this, but determined to try to make things seem 'normal' for Mum, and so wanted to be at the hospital with her as much as he could, especially for all meal times We knew we had to make that possible for him.

Our circumstances were such that Anne and I managed the bulk of the weekday 'shifts' at this time, as we weren't working. John could do weekends, Sue's days-off were a Sunday (after church) and Monday, so she covered those, as well as taking the odd day off work to fill in. Rick had just had major surgery himself, so was unable to travel, let alone help out with Dad. Bearing in mind that the Manchester contingent had a one and a half hour drive to Morecambe, and for me it was two and a half hours, setting up the rota was no mean feat. But between us we drove Dad to the hospital twice daily, spent time with Mum, drank lots of tea in the canteen ringing round the rest of the family with updates, and made sure Dad was never alone, eating and resting well when he was at home.

The following week, Mum was healing well physically, but there was little change in her confusion. And if this wasn't bad enough, one morning Dad took a phone call to let him know that his sister had passed away – not unexpected, but still incredibly upsetting. I happened to be with him that day, and once our hospital visits were over, it was clear that he was becoming increasingly unwell. The stress of the past fortnight, the news about his sister, the many car journeys to and from Lancaster hospital, had all taken their toll - our big, strong, gentle giant was now a broken man. Having had his world turned upside down, he had finally let down his guard and allowed the pains he had been refusing to acknowledge, take hold. At midnight, on advice from the district nurse, I piled him into the car and headed for A&E, where they kept him in for a few days for assessment.

So now, Mum was in one ward, Dad in the ward opposite, and we had to split our visits between them, literally crossing paths and swapping notes in the corridor. Dad was clearly more unwell than any of us had realised. He had been so adamant that he had to look after Mum, that he had obviously neglected his own health, ignored the signs and symptoms, not confided in any of us, until the events of the last two weeks had brought about the perfect storm. He was allowed home after a few days, with the promise of an operation due in a couple of weeks' time, which at 88 years old was daunting to say the least. Mum was discharged once Dad reluctantly agreed to accept some outside help, as he wasn't currently strong enough to manage on his own, and Mum's needs were now significantly more challenging than before her fall. The care package on offer was pretty minimal, and although we were all tired and emotionally drained, we couldn't stand back and watch Dad try to cope while he was so ill. So the rota just drifted on, with us all taking turns to drive up the M6 and spend a couple of days with them, before the next one of us took over.

When the time came for Dad's operation, we had to 'up' the rota, so that two of us were there most of the time. Mum needed 24 hour supervision, and Dad needed visitors, so we simply got on with it. But once he was home recuperating, it began to dawn on us that for the foreseeable future, we would need two of us with them for most of the time, to help with all of their needs until Dad was back to strength. There were just a few weeks to go before Christmas, and we were all shattered, so with our own families to think about, we broached the subject of respite care for them both. With a heavy heart, and purely because he could see that we were all beginning to struggle, Dad agreed to a four-week stay with Mum in a care home in Manchester, where most of us, and the wider family could visit more easily.

Had we had the luxury of a crystal ball, we would never have suggested this, but selfishly, we all needed a break, some breathing space and family time, and we honestly thought Dad might enjoy the rest as well. He didn't. Exactly four weeks later, early in the New Year, we moved them back into their home in Morecambe. We didn't yet set up the rota as such, just made sure that one of us could visit every few days to do the shopping, washing etc, and see how Dad was coping.

It was on one such visit towards the end of January that Anne was shocked to see Dad when he opened the door to her. He was clearly very unwell. He had reluctantly come to the decision that he could no longer manage to look after Mum, and he obviously needed to see a doctor as a matter of urgency. We jumped in straight away. I trawled the internet from home and called all the care homes in Morecambe, whilst Anne dealt with Dad's immediate medical issues. To cut a long and painful story short, we managed to find a bed in the only care home in the area with immediate availability, and which could provide for Mum's needs. A couple of days later, Sue had the awful task of driving them both to the home, and only driving one of them back.

Dad was devastated, and two days later, having only managed to visit Mum once, he was taken into hospital. The rota was resurrected so we could visit Dad, and spend time with Mum while she settled in her new home. Foolishly, I decided I could fit my cycle training in around all of this – I still had my trip in May to prepare for, and needed to put in the miles. When it was my shift, I would cycle to the care home in the morning to see Mum, cycle back, drive to the hospital for the afternoon visiting, drive back and cycle a bit more, before heading back to the hospital for the evening visit. After that, it would be time for food and ringing round the family before bed – a hectic schedule. But we all took our turns, including Rick who by now was well enough to travel and help out.

After a week or so, Dad was finally diagnosed. It was a Friday, and I had left mid-afternoon to try to beat the traffic. John was driving up after work for the evening visiting, and there didn't seem the need for an overlap. In the gap between me leaving and John arriving, the doctors had given Dad his test results, and it wasn't good news. Why did I rush away? We were planning on spending the weekend with Rebecca and James, so I was keen to miss rush hour and make it to their flat in time to go out for dinner. Hindsight is a wonderful thing, but you can only imagine how much I regret not being with him when the doctor came that day. If only I'd known...

John had the dreadful task of ringing round that night with the news that Dad had cancer, it was inoperable, and he had just a few weeks left.

I think we were all at the hospital the following Monday, when there was to be a meeting with the palliative care team, to discuss what came next. In that time, we had all begun to take in the news, although I'm not sure that Dad fully comprehended the situation. At the meeting, all the options were outlined, and Dad chose to spend his last few weeks at home in Morecambe, with the care package on offer. It was a very comprehensive care package, with a hospital bed set up downstairs, a team of carers popping in 3 times a day, district nurses and hospice nurses on call, and a direct 'bat-phone' to the local surgery. We again set up the rota, and this time we were all fully involved. Rick was pretty much fully recovered and could run his business online from Morecambe if he had to, John had put his workload on hold as best he could, and Sue took time off on compassionate grounds. We took turns in being with Dad, visiting Mum when we could, and ringing round each evening with an update.

I don't know why I hesitated at first, but just before Dad came out of hospital, I asked Bob to call Peak Tours to cancel my bike ride – I was unable to talk coherently about our circumstances to many people outside of the family, and bizarrely I felt a mixture of emotions. Firstly, cheated that the adventure I had imagined for the last four years was no longer happening, and then enormous guilt that I felt that way. After all, I could ride my bike anytime, but time was the only thing I didn't have much of left with Dad. Peak Tours were great – but I insisted they keep my deposit as incentive to book again when I felt ready. I also had to let my friend Debbie know, as we were meant to be riding this together. She was one of my soulmates, and I often called her to offload about Mum and

Dad, so I don't think she was at all surprised, and she went on to do the trip anyway, with her husband. So with this decision made, I could concentrate on what was really important.

As in all such cases, Dad had been discharged with a carrier bag full of drugs. We kept a diary of what he'd had and when, so that we didn't accidentally overdose him when we were changing shifts, and also so Dad could be as comfortable as possible with the available pain management. In one of the kitchen cupboards, we stored the controlled drugs that could only be administered by a nurse, but which needed to be kept on hand - just in case. We christened this the 'scary cupboard' – we all knew what was in there, but none of us wanted to have to call upon the contents during our watch. It was a source of amusement to us all, especially Rick, who couldn't even bring himself to open the scary cupboard door unless a nurse was present! At first, we could manage Dad's needs single-handed, but latterly this progressed to two of us there at all times, in some ways as an emotional crutch for each other, as well as with the physical demands of caring for Dad.

It probably sounds bizarre, but those few weeks were certainly not all doom and gloom. Dad had an amazing sense of humour, and the situation we all found ourselves in threw up many golden moments of laughter. We were able to talk about the fantastic times we'd all had together, discuss plans for his funeral, and also look at what plans he would like for Mum's funeral, when her time came. All of his life, he had been a strong, patient, caring man, and as he faced his last challenge, he did so with a courage and dignity which I can only admire. But there were also some very dark days, and we all found the responsibility of caring for Dad difficult at times. The lack of sleep, the emotional turmoil and the desperate sadness, all took their toll, and at times we didn't always agree on what was best for Dad. However, the five of us had spent so much time with each other, calling or texting daily for months now, crying together lots, laughing at times, and it had brought us very much closer – something which Dad would have been immensely pleased with. Our hand-carved plaques bearing the inscription 'Family' now felt a little more special.

When Dad passed away, Anne, John and Sue were all with him.

I didn't make it in time. John had called to suggest I should drive up, so Bob had taken the wheel, and we were flying up the M6. Strangely, at 13.44 I looked at the dashboard clock, and couldn't stop the tears from welling. I knew then that I would be too late.

After the initial arrangements, we all went our separate ways, knowing that what we had done for Dad was exactly what he had wanted – to spend his last weeks at home surrounded by family. We had things to do, a funeral to prepare, families to spend time with. We could take a little time out, re-group for the funeral, and think about what to do about Mum. We had promised Dad that we would look after her, move her nearer to the family in Manchester, and find her the lovely home she deserved. Their GP advised us not to tell her about Dad, in case it was too distressing, and so the day after Dad died, I visited Mum before driving home, trying to appear as 'normal' as I could. It was a beautifully sunny day, and the carers brought round ice cream for everyone – Mum was smiling and happy, and it was reassuring to know that she had no idea of what Dad had been through.

The very next morning, having enjoyed my first night at home without sleeping with my phone on the bedside table, I was enjoying a cup of tea in bed when I heard ringing downstairs at 8.30. It was Anne. Mum had had a suspected stroke as they were getting her dressed at the home, and was on her way to hospital.

Again, Anne and Sue were the first on the scene, along with their husbands, and I waited at home until they had assessed the situation. When the call came at lunchtime, it was clear that things were pretty bad, so I hastily packed a bag and set off, not really knowing what I would find when I arrived. Her stroke had been catastrophic. In the whirlwind which was the next couple of days, the doctors came to the heart-breaking decision that Mum wouldn't recover, and the best we could do for her would be to withdraw all intervention, save for those drugs which kept her comfortable, and wait for nature to take its course.

The rota was resurrected, but it was very different this time. We could see that this wouldn't be for long, and there was little we could do apart from hold her hand, talk to her, and be her family. This time we didn't really take turns as such. We were there whenever we wanted to be, and often overlapped. It was good to have each other to lean on as we kept up the bedside vigil and she was never alone, except for overnight, and sometimes not even then. There was a very different atmosphere around Mum's bed. With Dad, there had been laughter, reminiscing, happy times. With Mum, there was simply overwhelming sadness.

I was with her when she passed away very peacefully, after two and a half weeks of fighting. They were together again, and Dad hadn't had the trauma of seeing her after her stroke. We take great comfort from that.

Aside from becoming closer to my brothers and sisters, the one good thing to come from all of this was that we could now give Mum and Dad a joint funeral - and Dad had planned a lot of it for us. We were all very much involved. We needed 12 pall bearers, and there was no shortage of volunteers from the immediate family. They were led by John and Rick, who were at the head of Dad's coffin on the way into church, and of Mum's on the way out. Rick wrote the eulogy with a little input from us all. He didn't dwell on the usual chronological list of events in their lives, but instead stressed their incredibly strong family values, how they touched so many peoples' lives, and most importantly their devotion to each other. The tribute was good, from the heart, and summed up what was the most important thing to them both – family. I volunteered to read the eulogy with one of my nephews, and although I'm not the best public speaker in the world, I hope I did the words justice. Another nephew read a passage from the Bible, Sue wrote and read the prayers and words of thanks, and Anne read two beautiful poems at the crematorium.

We all feel immensely proud that we did a great job of the funeral, and if they were looking down that day, they would have loved it – the church was packed. After almost 70 years of marriage, it seemed a very fitting last waltz together...

It was now late May, and this had been my 50th year - the year I had had such big plans for. Things hadn't quite turned out the way I'd expected, but it had certainly been eventful. In the space of just 10 months, we had sold the business, left our home of 21 years, started a new life in Shropshire, ridden the emotional rollercoaster of looking after Mum and Dad, and been to their joint funeral. We felt shell-shocked, battered and bruised.

I pushed the family to help empty the house three weeks later. It was never going to be an easy task, so it largely didn't make a difference whether we did it now or in six months' time, and they were all incredibly supportive. John had already sorted through Dad's greenhouses and garage whilst Mum was in hospital - a task that would have taken us a full week on its own, with everything he'd accumulated over the years! We managed to get the job done in one very long day, thanks to John's big empty van, all hands on deck, and a very helpful charity shop around the corner. Now Bob and I could put the house on the market, and close this chapter. Since Mum's fall, we had all been 'hot-bedding' in the spare rooms, and although the house provoked many happy memories from the last 17 years, it now also held ghosts. It took six months, but it sold at a realistic price, considering it was in dire need of modernising.

John had been nominated as executor for both wills, and he spent a few months of thorough work before the finances were settled, complicated by the fact that Mum hadn't survived Dad for long enough to benefit from his will. It became clear that

Dad had been a little too hasty in cashing in some of his investments all those years ago, as his bank balance was healthy – there was still some income, and at least one untouched savings account in place, and in recent years Mum and Dad had qualified for several state benefits. Dad had thought that all of his remaining money would be spent on Mum's care fees, and that there wouldn't be anything left in the coffers for his family – sadly, he needn't have worried.

Moving Forwards

And so we could all begin to look to the future. Bob and I spent some of our inheritance on a wonderful holiday with Rebecca, James and Cameron in the Loire valley. For once, we vowed we would do all the things we wanted to, without looking at the price tag – hire bikes and canoes, see all the sights, eat out every day, and drink good wine! Each evening we would raise a glass of something very pleasant indeed, to Granny and Grandad. Mum and Dad would have loved that we used it for real family time!

We began to re-charge the batteries, grieve properly, and finally start to put down roots in our new home town. Slowly but surely, we could feel almost normal, and get on with life. I missed the daily interaction with my brothers and sisters at first, but we soon got back on to the more usual track of speaking to each other when we fancied it, or when there was something to say. This was a record-breaking summer of pretty solid sunshine and high temperatures, and we enjoyed it to the full, with barbeques a-plenty. We did a bit of cycling and walking, nothing too strenuous, but it was a very good summer, and just what the doctor ordered after such an ordeal. In amongst all of this, James had proposed to Rebecca whilst they were on a mini-break at St Andrews, and she had happily accepted. We now had a wedding to plan for, outfits to choose – life was beginning to be good again.

And my thoughts soon turned towards re-booking my bike ride. For obvious reasons, Peak Tours don't run trips through the winter, so I looked to the following year, when I would be

51 and three quarters! Better late than never... I wasn't fit, slim or motivated to get back on my bike, but I figured that booking the trip would be the incentive I needed, and as I was discussing dates with Bob, he suggested that maybe this time he could come with me. I admit I didn't jump for joy straight away – this had always been MY thing, MY challenge, and I had really enjoyed the freedom of travelling and experiencing the LeJog trip on my own. However, things were different this time, and the thought of sharing the trip with the one person who had been by my side throughout the last 28 years, and who had been so very supportive in the recent traumatic times, was enormously appealing. This would be a wonderful experience, and maybe we should treat it as more of a holiday than a challenge; taking in the sights, smells and sounds throughout the length of France.

My main reservation was that we don't cycle together very often, and we have very different styles of riding, normally resulting in me pedalling half a mile behind, demoralised and trying to catch up! Bob is not a social cyclist, and sees any outdoor pursuit as a form of exercise – to be done at full pelt. But he assured me that we would train and ride as a team, and so we booked for the following June. This should give us plenty of time to get fitter after Christmas, and then start the official training programme in late March.

The Training

In order to fully enjoy the ride, and to minimise the risk of injury, we knew that we needed to be pretty fit before we embarked on cycling such a distance, and we took our exercise regime seriously. We joined a gym in mid-November, which would mean that we had no excuses to slack through the winter, whatever the weather, and then by mid-March, we'd be able to make the most of the (hopefully) better conditions, ditch the gym, and get out regularly on the bikes.

As well as very different styles of riding, it transpired that we also have differing systems when it comes to gym workouts. Bob mostly spent his time pushing hard on the static bikes, and he lost weight quickly. My weight loss was slower, though I used a variety of cardio machines, but I was certainly getting stronger, and feeling very confident that I would be fitter than I was before I set out to conquer LeJog. After all, we were going to the gym four times a week, which was way more exercise than I've ever done since my time in the RAF!

We were blessed with a very mild winter, so we ventured out on the bikes at times too, but this initially wasn't as successful as it should have been. It took us a good many short rides and several heated 'discussions' before we found a system of riding together which suited us both, but by the time it clicked, we were indeed riding as a team, and ready to tackle the miles required for our training programme.

We had also been on a one-day bike maintenance course, and were now fairly confident that we could manage most issues with our bikes, including full services and replacing worn parts. There were a couple of problems that might crop up which we'd have to seek help for, but generally we could now keep our bikes in very good working order, and fix most small niggles at the roadside.

As on my previous venture, Peak Tours had suggested a 10-week training programme, designed to take us from a base level to being ready for the trip, and I had taken this as a guide and enhanced it greatly! Our problem was that we now live in one of the flattest parts of the UK, and we needed long hills in our training to replicate the type of terrain we would encounter in France. We could put in some flat rides of a longer distance than suggested by Peak Tours, to compensate for the lack of climbing, or we could pop the bikes in the car and drive to hillier locations. I planned to do both.

We had set distance rides to do each week, gradually increasing in length and ascent, and suffice to say that our training went really well. As we were still in our 'gap year', we could pick and choose which days we would cycle according to the weather forecast, and coupled with a very mild and dry spring, we managed to enjoy the majority of our training in fabulous conditions. It was lovely to be out cycling regularly again, especially in countryside which was all new to us, and we felt very fortunate not to have to fit the miles in around working hours.

When we rode near to home in the spring, fields of rape with its strong aroma and vibrant colour surrounded us, and when we headed into the Welsh hills, our senses were hit by the abundant wild garlic and dramatic scenery. We passed farms with tiny new-born lambs, and weeks later we'd watch them jumping and playing in groups, and newly planted fields soon became lush and green. Time flew by. We did have to ride in the wet a few times, but this was useful in testing our bad weather kit, which turned out to be pretty inadequate! We didn't buy any new gear – just kept everything crossed that there wouldn't be much wet weather in France...

There were a couple of weeks where life got in the way, and we didn't manage the full mileage I had set, but my training programme was ambitious, and in the grand scheme of things it didn't really matter that we couldn't always fulfil my targets. The distractions we had during this period of time were good ones, and compared to the previous year, life in our household was simply great.

Rebecca and James had decided to get married at the university chapel in St Andrews, the town which meant so much to them both. The date was set for early August, and preparations were well underway. They knew exactly how they wanted their big day to be, and kept us updated as they made all their arrangements. It had been a lovely experience shopping for wedding dresses with Rebecca, some much cherished mother-and-daughter time, and the dress she had chosen was perfect for her. They were happy and excited, and it was a joy to ride the wave with them – everyone in the family was looking forward to sharing their big day.

Cameron had decided that when his contract finished at Wells in the summer, he would enrol on a Masters course in order to improve the chances of achieving his goal of employment in an orchestra. As tuition fees in the UK were prohibitive, he looked to universities overseas, and aimed high – applying first to Yale, and then to Amsterdam as his Plan B. Competition was fierce from applicants worldwide, and Yale had an intake of just three post-grad flute students, but after submitting his audition videos, he was called forward to the live selection and offered a two-year scholarship: a truly amazing achievement. He also secured a place on the course at Amsterdam, but graciously declined – Yale was too good an opportunity to miss out on! It was equally joyous to see him so happy, his confidence blooming as he began to plan for his new life in the USA. Rebecca and Cameron both now had a very bright future to look forward to, and Mum and Dad would have been immensely proud.

And so with one week to go, bikes fully serviced, 1420 miles covered with 66,320ft of climbs in the last 10 weeks alone, I think we were ready. One thing was quite different this time. On my last trip I relished the personal challenge and was determined to pedal every inch of the way, ending up a little disappointed when that hadn't worked out. This time I was much more relaxed, my main goal was to make the most of the whole experience, and it wouldn't matter one little bit if I got off to push up the odd steep hill! My training programme had a much-needed week of rest built in before we set off for the ferry at Portsmouth, but during that week, there was the small matter of Rebecca's hen weekend. Still, I needed some drinking training too, and just for good measure, I did a bit of karaoke practice at the same time – well, you never know... The weekend was the most magical experience, with 12 ladies in a large lakeside house, enough food and drink for a fortnight, laughter, and many special memories.

Channel to the Med

The day before we were to travel had been set aside as our 'packing day'. Our bikes were already with Peak Tours, and we would be reunited with them at the start line, so all that remained was to sort out our cycling kit and evening clothes. Being the hopelessly organised person that I am, meant we had everything ready in advance and simply had to squash it all into suitcases. That left us with time on our hands, so we flicked on the TV to watch the 75th anniversary commemorations of the D-Day landings. The services were really quite moving, and a fitting tribute to all those who lost their lives for our freedom. It seemed a timely coincidence that the coverage was broadcast from the coastline where we would be setting off on our adventure in a couple of days.

I also had a hospital appointment to attend, for the results of some tests I'd had recently, following a problem which had cropped up during our training. Despite being pretty fit now, I found that hard exercise, whether it be pushing myself at the gym, or cycling up very steep hills, left me uncomfortably breathless, my heart-rate racing higher than ever before, often dizzy, and with occasional stich-like chest pains. The tests so far showed nothing physically abnormal, but the symptoms apparently suggested angina, and I would need further tests. Having explained the 'holiday' I was about to embark on, I was told to carry on as normal, but to listen to my body, and if I became uncomfortable, to stop and rest until the symptoms passed fully before continuing. The medics assured me that I was unlikely to make anything worse if I followed their advice.

Having looked forward to this ride for five years, I wasn't going to let a little medical hiccup worry me, and was keen to get going.

I had a fitful night's sleep, frequently waking to check whether it was time to go, but then we were up, ready, and in the hire car to Portsmouth by 7am. There was a storm heading north from France, and we hit torrential rain as soon as we neared Portsmouth, but we still arrived with time to spare. Our meeting point was a pub near the ferry-port, and there we found a few other Peak Tours cyclists already sipping beer. They were all male, save for another couple, Trevor and Vicky, and I was relieved to see that there would be at least one other female sharing the journey. We all made polite chat, discussed previous Peak Tours trips, and it was reassuring to hear that they mostly had good northern accents!

Because of the strong winds forecast – in excess of 40mph – our ferry was delayed, and for the same reason, I chose to take a motion sickness pill and forego the alcohol which was tempting me from every angle. Thankfully, the forecast was for this storm to blow through quickly, but unfortunately not until after our crossing. Once in Ouistreham, we had a short battle against the elements to reach the ferry-port hotel, and try to get some sleep in the hot, stuffy room, before breakfast in the morning.

Day 1. Ouistreham to Bagnoles de L'Orne
Miles – 68
Ascent – 3421ft
Average Speed – 11.2mph
Calories – 3433

After a pretty good night's sleep we ventured down for breakfast, and had the privilege to be sharing the dining room with a few of the veterans who had been at the D-Day anniversary commemorations. They put us to shame, immaculately dressed in suit and tie, proudly displaying their medals and being the perfect gentlemen, whilst we noisy cyclists in our lycra attacked the buffet breakfast like locusts. It was humbling to be in the presence of some of the men whose bravery meant we can now jump on our bikes and cycle the length of France at our leisure. Bob made a point of shaking their hands.

We were meant to have a briefing at 8.30, but the scenes outside the hotel were a tad chaotic. Bob and I found our bikes quickly and were keen to go, but others had problems getting their bikes and Garmins (a type of bike satnav) ready for the off. In one case, an issue with a bike that had cropped up a couple of days before was now causing a delay whilst the Peak Tours mechanic attempted to do a quick fix. The storm had indeed passed, but there were still strong winds, and it was nippy standing around waiting to set off, but after what seemed like an age, we all cycled round the corner to the official start point at the Charles De Gaulle monument. As it was so cold, the morning brief was kept mercifully short and there was just time for a quick team photo before we began our adventure.

For some bizarre reason, I found myself leading the pack along the cycle path following the Caen canal, chief navigator and pace-setter. That would turn out to be the one and only time I would be in the lead for the entire length of France!

After a couple of miles the others began to overtake, until we arrived at Pegasus Bridge, where we stopped to take photos. Pegasus Bridge was one of the main objectives for the troops who had landed on Sword Beach exactly 75 years ago, and was featured in the movie 'The Longest Day'. It was very moving to witness veterans and their families watching the bridge as it opened to let boat traffic through, and lucky we had been delayed at the start, or we may have missed that opportunity. Had our trip not coincided with the 75th anniversary, I might never have known the true significance of this moveable lump of metal spanning the canal, but seeing the moist eyes of the veterans, and their relatives bursting with pride, hammered it home.

Pressing onwards against a dying headwind, we were now on a blissfully flat cycle path following the canal, although it was strewn with debris from the previous day's storm, and a couple of people picked up punctures. After navigating through the outskirts of Caen, we were back onto a silky smooth cycle path which followed a disused railway line through woodland, occasionally criss-crossing the rails as we went. Despite the threat of rain, I was loving this! It was just how I imagined French cycling to be, and I was secretly hoping the whole journey would be traffic-free.

By late morning we left the railway behind and progressed onto quiet back lanes which threaded through tiny hamlets and villages - some well-kept, some less-so - following the River

Orne as it meandered through the surrounding hillsides. This was all still countryside which would have been teeming with troops 75 years ago, and I'm sure that the landscape hasn't changed significantly. Lunch today was at a riverside café, obviously popular for water-sports in the high season, but today there were no takers for the pedalos - just us cyclists looking for nourishment. With good, quick service and hearty food, we were soon ready for the off, deciding to keep our rain jackets on for the afternoon as the sky looked threatening – a very wise move! The roads were again empty and smooth, undulating not hilly, and dotted with pockets of civilisation, but the threat soon turned very real and there were a few really heavy showers. It had been a while since I last saw rain this intense, so bad that we took shelter under a tall bridge waiting for the deluge to pass, and for the newly-formed rivers on the roads to subside.

For the latter part of the day we were approaching a national park, and the terrain became slightly hillier, although nothing to make me breathe too heavily. The roads were straighter and wider, but still remarkably quiet, and we could clearly see marked footpaths off into the forests. Since Pegasus Bridge, Bob and I had cycled most of the day together on our own, catching up with the others at the brew-stops. I had known all along that I would probably end up the slowest at the back again, but I was going to wear this as a badge of honour, preferring to cycle at a pace I could keep up comfortably all day, and fully enjoying my surroundings. I felt that somehow we got better value for money if we were cycling for longer! Bob could quite easily have pedalled ahead with the others, but we were riding as a team, and he held back and stayed with me - it didn't really matter how long it took.

We arrived in the very pretty spa town of Bagnoles de L'Orne for our first night's stop, a town famed for its therapeutic thermal baths, and interesting architecture. We rode into town past once-magnificent buildings, clearly huge spa hotels, but which were now beyond their best and appeared to be apartments. However, the centre of town was still gloriously picturesque, and we enjoyed a jug of the local cider with the other riders before dinner together in the hotel.

This was our 'welcome' evening, where we were issued with our Peak Tours cycle jerseys, and introduced to the tour guides properly. There was Rob, currently leading the team, but who would be leaving in two days to be replaced by their usual tour leader. Alberto, the bike mechanic, who would take turns with Dylan to ride 'sweep' at the back, to mop up anyone who had mechanical or other problems. As per LeJog, there were the red vans (or 'van rouges' in France!) providing a mid-morning and mid-afternoon brew-stop for refreshments, and a lunch stop which would hopefully be a picnic in the lovely weather. They would double as the luggage transfers and support vehicles if required.

It was a very pleasant evening sitting at a large table getting to know some of the other cyclists, although the talk was still mostly of previous Peak Tours trips, Garmins and bikes. But we seemed to gravitate towards Trevor and Vicky, whom we'd met in Portsmouth, and we progressed quickly beyond the small talk, and onto testing out each other's sense of humour. They appeared to be very good company!

Day 2. Bagnoles de L'Orne to La Fleche
Miles – 79.5
Ascent – 4189ft
Average Speed – 11.62mph
Calories – 4197

The hotel in Bagnoles had been lovely, with stunning views of the lake from our bedroom window and a really nice breakfast buffet. It was cloudy today, but thankfully dry and after our morning brief, we set off towards the front of the pack, but by the first brew-stop we were already bringing up the rear. The morning saw us cycle through Calvados country, and I thought we'd see more orchards. Instead it was quite heavily forested through the national park, but lovely long gentle climbs and descents on eerily quiet lanes with barely any traffic to contend with, meant that I was still thoroughly enjoying pootling along at the back with Bob. We passed a couple of chateaux early on, one in particular just outside Bagnoles was surrounded by beautifully coloured rhododendron bushes in full bloom, all reflected in the mirror-like lake on which it nestled – simply stunning.

We were still in the national park by lunchtime, which today was by the side of a lake, at a café set on a sandy beach within the forest. Most of the others had arrived long before us and were getting ready to leave as we sat down to read the menu, but Trevor and Vicky ate with us, and again we chatted and laughed, before setting off together for the afternoon's ride.

The route flattened out now and we rode undisturbed along country roads, dotted with villages which announced themselves from the distance with their tall slender church spires. We whizzed through places with delicious sounding names like St Symphorien and St Cyr en Pail (who I'm reliably informed is not the patron saint of buckets), and each village marked your arrival and departure with a tall crucifix. This must be, or have been, a very religious part of France, churches and crosses being the focal point of the villages, but on this particular Sunday there were few signs of life, save for dogs barking and chasing us from behind their fences as we passed. The houses were mostly well-kept and I could clearly smell bergamot and other scented flowers growing in gardens as we quietly drifted by. This was rural France at its beautiful best, sleepy and green, and the surrounding countryside was agricultural with fields of crops edged with poppies. I couldn't help smiling as we pedalled along, happy that this trip was proving to be everything I had hoped for, and excited at the prospect of what was to come.

We seemed to have been heading directly south for the most part today, barely making any turns, and the last 10 miles or so were up a gentle incline to the busy town of La Fleche. We had at last begun to see the large-scale commercial orchards I had imagined, with row upon row of carefully maintained trees, often covered with nets to protect their precious harvest. The mileage had been high today and this last stretch felt like a bit of a slog, so inevitably we dropped back a little from the others and had been caught up by Alberto. We got chatting about life in general, and the miles ticked by until we arrived at our hotel. It had been a long day in the saddle, so I opted not to have the post-ride beer with the others which had so quickly become tradition, choosing instead to inspect the inside of my eyelids for a short while…

That evening there wasn't much open in La Fleche as it was Sunday, but Peak Tours had arranged for the restaurant opposite the hotel to provide us with dinner. We had pre-ordered from a set menu to help them with their planning, but when we arrived, it was pretty chaotic. La Patronne was very flustered despite our tour guides having print-outs of what everyone had ordered, and there was much arm waving and raised voices. Dylan stepped in to the rescue, calm as ever, ensuring we all got what we wanted, but it took a lot longer than it should and most of us went straight to bed after dinner. We had spent the evening sitting with, amongst others, the third couple on the trip who were from Iceland, and we were now fluent in how to say 'cheers' in Icelandic! Skàl!

Day 3. La Fleche to Loches
Miles – 79.5 (or 62 as it turned out!)
Ascent – 3280ft
Average Speed – 13mph
Calories – 3162

It had rained very heavily in the night, and continued to do so at breakfast, thankfully easing by morning brief. Today was the one day we would have no 'sweep', as Rob was returning to the UK, and our new tour leader Isabelle, would meet us in Loches this evening. We left La Fleche along a traffic-free cycle path, but were soon back on single-track roads through countryside and villages similar to yesterday. Architecture aside, the rolling hills and green fields we passed this morning could quite easily have been in the UK, and although the scenery was nice, it wasn't 'special' or different. That said, it certainly beat working for a living, and I found I was still smiling as the miles drifted by.

Shortly after the first brew-stop we passed into serious farming country, with commercial orchards boasting hundreds of rows of netted trees laden with young apples, pears and plums. The scenery soon opened out into vast swathes of arable crops - corn, wheat, rape, sunflowers, barley, and all edged with poppies and cornflowers, looking spectacular. It wasn't hilly, but as we were slowly plodding up a gentle incline, I heard a metallic ping, and realised I had snapped a front spoke. This normally shouldn't be a problem, but in my case the wheel had warped, and wouldn't turn without catching on the frame and brake calipers. Really annoying, as the wheel was less than a month old! But I couldn't ride it in this state, and as there was no sweep to help, we had to call Alberto who had passed us in the brew van not many minutes before. He turned the van around, loaded up my bike, and we drove the 17 miles to the lunch stop, where the other van would have spares. Bob happily cycled on at a much faster pace to try to catch up with the others, pleased to be able to stretch his legs.

That was that, then! My End-to-End wouldn't be, as I would now always be 17 miles short of the full distance. I was disappointed, but it was completely unavoidable, and I had to keep reminding myself that my priority was experiencing France, and not being too hung up about pedalling every inch of the way. Alberto drove me along the route I should have cycled, and it was really picturesque, passing through some larger but prettier towns. In this area, they all seem to be 'Villages Fleuri', and someone puts a lot of time and effort into keeping them in bloom. At one point we drove along a section of single-track road, maybe for 2 miles, which was pot-holed and with a very rough surface. I really didn't mind missing the pounding that my backside and wrists would have taken along this stretch - it was bumpy enough in the van! This road led to the busy town of Langeais, with its imposingly beautiful chateau standing dominant in the centre, and although I've seen inside many a chateau, it looked very inviting. Around the town centre there were cobbled streets, cars and tourists to contend with, so again, it wasn't all bad being chauffeur driven!

Lunch was a picnic by the side of the mighty River Loire, in an idyllic location overlooking the bridge we were to cross by – hard to believe we'd reached this far south through France in just two and a half days. Alberto quickly swapped my wheel for one of the spares the support van carries, and then helped Dylan to serve the picnic lunch, promising that my wheel would have a new spoke as soon as he could find one that fitted. Bob arrived only minutes after the tail-enders, and had really enjoyed blasting along the relatively flat route.

After lunch, I test-rode my new wheel up the climb away from the river. This was the area where we'd spent our family holiday (and Mum and Dad's money) last year, and we knew we were heading towards chateaux territory. We briefly stopped for photos at Azay-Le-Rideau, allegedly famed for being the inspiration for Sleeping Beauty's castle in the Disney film, and where we'd had a lovely picnic when we last visited, but there were several more hugely impressive buildings along the route. It beggars belief that there was such wealth in this area, to merit the construction of such majestic and magnificent homes all those years ago; their upkeep today must be staggering. We passed signs for the Troglodyte Valley, where at the other end of the scale, people lived in dwellings carved from the rocks, but we opted not to detour off route to visit.

We passed the occasional vineyard and more large-scale orchards, until we found the brew van for our break, before the final leg to Loches. I'm not going to say that during the late afternoon the scenery was boring, just 'samey'. The roads were wider, busier, the villages bigger and not so pretty, and there was more evidence of industry, rather than just agriculture. As it was flat and not too hot, we pressed on quickly, but after such amazing sights so far, and now with little to catch our eye, it seemed uneventful.

Our night stop was at Loches, a place we knew well having stayed there with the family last year, and where we had pre-booked a table for four at our favourite restaurant in the town. We had assumed that by day three, we would know someone well enough to invite them to join us, and Trevor and Vicky fitted the bill. We had a very pleasant evening getting to know them properly, away from the crowds, and enjoying a special meal a bit more 'upmarket' than we'd had thus far. After dinner we took a stroll around the medieval royal city before retiring to bed, and it felt like we had known our new friends for ages, not just three days. A lovely evening, in great company!

Day 4. Loches to Crozant

Miles – 72

Ascent – 3020ft

Average Speed – 11.38

Calories – 3599

Our hotel was quirky to say the least, and had a 16th century wooden staircase winding upwards through the middle. This ancient feature was open to the elements on one side, so it was remarkable that it had stood the test of time. Breakfast was equally bizarre. Our host made tea and coffee behind a tall desk shrouded with a curtain, reminiscent of a Victorian Punch & Judy show, and we expected him to announce "That's the way to do it!" every time he poured coffee! The dining room was strewn with books and artefacts obviously aimed at the literary clientele, and the crockery and cutlery were the vintage shabby chic kind, where nothing matched, and the china felt paper thin.

After breakfast we headed out for our first morning brief with our new tour leader, Isabelle. Though small in stature, she had huge presence and a beaming smile - a wonderfully warm blend of schoolteacher, mother hen and friend. She worked hard over the next couple of days to make up for lost time, quickly learning all our names and foibles. Her immortal words were "Keep your head up and look around you. The tarmac looks the same all over the world!", and with this mantra echoing through our helmets, we were off.

Again it had rained overnight, so we wore coats for the first leg of the day, and set off at the back of the pack from the start, through farmland and past several chateaux which sadly had seen better days. It was well-known now amongst our fellow riders, that Bob and I would be bringing up the rear all the time, but this morning we seemed to be gaining ground on one of the others. He was clearly having an off day, and was plodding slowly up a hill when we caught him up. I had a dilemma – should we overtake him as he was at a slower pace than even I wanted to ride, or would that make him feel a whole lot worse? There can be nothing more demoralising than seeing me creep past on a hill. But pass him we did and we were again cycling along narrow lanes through fields of knee-high corn, the small farmsteads advertising foie gras for sale to the public – obviously how they use any leftover corn. Today's route would see us undulating slightly upwards all day, making the going slower and more tiring, and ending the day with our first taste of real hills.

From the arable fields of the morning, we crossed through another national park, with well surfaced paths off into the woods, clearly used by walkers and mountain bikers. At around 26 miles the sky turned black with the promise of rain, and sure enough, the heavens opened. We stopped briefly to shelter under a tree, allowing the new backmarker to overtake us and Alberto to catch up, but soon realised the rain was set in for quite some time, and we had to move on regardless. The road surface was very good, smooth tarmac and wider now, but also a little busier than we were used to, with lots of spray. There was still quite some distance to cover before the lunch stop, so I tucked my head down and pressed on as hard as I was comfortable with, towards what should have been our picnic lunch on the village green, but was now an indoor picnic in a local café. Bob and Alberto chatted away behind me, but we were all soaked through, and it felt like a chore.

The others were all in the café when we arrived, and had dripped dry a little. There was nowhere left to sit, just a sea of soaked cyclists, and nowhere to hang our coats. My face must have been a picture, as a number of them stood to offer their seat, but thankfully a few hardy souls started getting ready for the off, allowing Bob and I to spread out a little. Trevor and Vicky were reluctant to leave in the heavy rain, so we sat with them sipping hot drinks, hoping that it would soon ease. We had got to know them well enough by now, that we'd had a few funny and frank discussions about the state of some of the French toilets. After Bob had paid a visit I quizzed him as to whether there was toilet paper in the café's facilities, and was able to nudge Vicky and quietly report to her that indeed there was! Her eyes lit up like a child's on Christmas morning – it's the simple pleasures... But we couldn't stay there all day enjoying ourselves, drinking coffee and making excuses to use the loo, so we left as the rain began to lift, and thankfully it stopped after another 10 miles.

Things were much more scenic now, following the River Creuse upstream as it flowed silently onwards. We crossed beautiful bridges, passed through larger towns and marvelled at imposing chateaux, reflected in the still waters of the wide river below. But with substantial rivers, come gorges and cols, and we had our first serious climb up to the afternoon brew van, where we chatted to Isabelle properly for the first time, waiting for yet another heavy shower to pass. She seemed lovely, had been tour leader on this trip many times, and so had stepped in easily.

From there we continued our climb up the valley and the road twisted and turned in a series of hairpins, before a lovely gradual descent towards our hotel. It was the kind of road I'd only ever seen on TV before, snaking up and down the steep sides of the valley, but which would soon become very much the 'norm'. As we freewheeled down through the wooded switchbacks, we heard a pack of hunting dogs in the forest off to our left, and I also caught a glimpse of a buzzard swooping down to catch its prey which squealed like a child. Quite pleased we were travelling too quickly to see what was going on in the undergrowth...

We eventually arrived, still dripping, at the aptly named Hotel Du Lac, overlooking a lake with boats and canoes for hire, and just beyond the ruins of a castle standing proudly on the hillside. As if a switch had been flicked, the sun popped out, and it became really warm – warm enough to sit out on the balcony for our post-ride drinks, whilst our lovely landlady offered to wash and dry all of our clothes.

Tonight, our group was split over three separate locations, owing to accommodation issues. Some had an early finish, but would have to pedal seven miles to reach us in the morning, whilst others had continued onwards for a further five miles today, and would be able to delay their start tomorrow until we all caught up. We were a group of 11, and it was definitely one of the most memorable evenings of the trip, getting to know them all, laughing and joking, eating duck a l'orange and probably drinking a glass or two too many....

Day 5. Crozant to Aubusson

Miles – 56
Ascent – 4012ft
Average Speed – 9.76mph
Calories – 3130

We awoke to torrential rain (again!), and ate a lovely breakfast watching huge droplets bounce onto the lake's surface. We were meant to have our morning briefing at 8.45, once the others had caught us up from the day before. Not wanting to delay us, they had set off in the downpour and arrived at our hotel drenched and understandably a little cross that we weren't in a rush to get going until this had passed. But get going we did, once the rain turned to drizzle, and - in waterproofs - we cycled up the steep road out of the valley. Today would see us climb steadily all day, with some steeper sections up and over small cols. We had to concentrate hard on the descents, as the heavy rain this morning had left debris and gravel on the roads, mostly on the bends.

We were in much hillier terrain now, still farmland, but the emphasis was on dairy rather than arable, as this region is noted for the Limousin cattle with their distinctive red colour and muscly form. They were out in force in the fields, and I was pleased that the fences separating us looked good and strong. Again we were on single track well-surfaced roads with little or no traffic, but passing through farmsteads rather than villages. Here the river had gouged out gorges from the surrounding hillsides, which looked quite dramatic, but a few more days of riding through this terrain, and we'd realise that they were really rather small! This would be the pattern of most of the cycling to come – long climbs up the hairpin bends to the top of the gorge, followed by a winding descent down the other side. However, the gradients were fairly gentle, certainly not as steep as the hills we'd covered during our training, and I found that if I dropped into my granny gear I could pedal up the ascents slowly enough to keep my breathing and heart rate at comfortable levels.

After a few miles we passed through Fresselines, and noticed the 'Monet Trail', a walk along the gorges passing several scenes which Monet painted when he spent time here. It's a very popular area for painters and art lovers, trying to capture the pure beauty of the Creuse valley, and I felt privileged to be able to see it in glimpses as we whizzed by.

Throughout the day we travelled through stone-built towns and villages which appeared older than most we'd seen thus far, and there was a spectacularly high viaduct across one gorge, which looked like it was closed and in need of repair. We were still following the Creuse, but it was much narrower now, and lining the river were the remains of industrial buildings and watermills. The area is also famed for its ancient oak trees, used to make brandy casks, and the valleys were heavily forested, providing us some shelter from the frequent showers.

Today was relatively low mileage, but the constant gradual ascent still made it feel like a long day in the saddle. The early afternoon stretch, especially, was against a headwind and the brew-stop couldn't come soon enough. When we arrived there, a number of our fellow cyclists were complaining about the weather, and about feeling tired, so that gave me a boost to know that I wasn't faring too badly after all! Where the van rouge was parked, however, couldn't have been prettier and was at one end of a lovely ancient stone bridge, looking up towards a medieval town with its church nestled into the hillside beyond. Had the sky been blue, it would have been a picture-postcard scene, and my spirits had lifted considerably by the time we pressed onwards to Aubusson.

This is a big town, and the heavier traffic came as a shock to the system after so many quiet miles, as did the road surface - which instantly deteriorates near to civilisation. I guess that the smooth tarmac on these rural lanes is entirely down to their lack of use. Although Aubusson was quite big, it had seen better days, and I chose not to join Bob for the post-ride beer in town. I was quite tired tonight, my legs still seemed fine, but I was just tired in general, and the long mileage so far, mostly in wet clothes, had caused a little chafing to my backside!

Cycling tours are a great leveller, and as we all were at dinner at the same restaurant that evening, there was much 'bottom' talk, which I joined in with heartily, swapping tips and tales, and generally happy to hear that it wasn't just me that was a little tender! Alberto and Dylan had joined us late, as they usually spent the early evening fixing any issues which had cropped up on anyone's bikes. They had been able to source spares in this town for a number of bikes with mechanical problems, and apparently my wheel was fixed, good as new. Bob and I had spent the evening sitting with Isabelle, and in her near-perfect English, she had explained that she had spent some time living and working in England, in exactly the area where I grew up – she was a fellow Mancunian, and we could now swap stories from 'home'! It's a small, small world at times…

Day 6. Aubusson to Le Mont Dore

Miles - 61
Ascent – 5966ft
Average Speed – 9.63mph
Calories – 3590

When Bob opened our curtains, we were met with an unfamiliar sight – sunshine! The mood was high amongst the cyclists at breakfast, and although we knew that this was billed as the day where the hills really began, to be dry and not in jackets would make life much more pleasant. Before the briefing I inspected my new spoke, which was silver against the other black ones, but gave me a bike with 'character', and the main thing was that the wheel turned perfectly. It also meant I again had my own smooth tyre, and not the deeper tread I'd had on the spare wheel - it's not much, but a little tread does give some vibration through the forks, which I hadn't really noticed until it was gone.

We were again on single track roads through forested valleys and gorges, but today the roads were covered with dappled sunlight, shining through the trees and warming us gently as we climbed. Everywhere carried the scent of fresh pine, and life felt really very good, Bob and I pedalling together at the back, thoroughly enjoying our ride. As we approached the town of Giat, we had our eyes peeled for road signs. Our village at home proudly declares 'Twinned with Giat' at every main road entrance, and we were keen to see if Giat was equally proud of its Shropshire sibling. We weren't disappointed - we had our picture taken by the sign, and stopped to take photos of the main bits of the town. It's probably bigger than Baschurch, but much prettier, and the most ironic thing was that just like us, they have a 'Spar' shop - open all hours!

There was a long shallow descent from Giat towards the lunch stop, and as Bob and I arrived in last, the others were all sitting outside a lovely roadside café in the sunshine, waiting. There was a procession of around 15 schoolkids from the primary school opposite, who filed past, politely saying 'bonjour' to us all, before being led into the café ahead of us. They obviously have their school dinner here each day, and were perfectly quiet and well behaved, despite the loud rabble of cyclists who piled in after them. It was a great place to eat, and they obviously have a good relationship with Peak Tours, having a large map of France on one wall with our route plotted and a 'you are here' dot, which we all studied from the queue for the (very nice!) loo.

However, we couldn't stay there enjoying ourselves too long - there were many more miles to cover in the lovely weather, so we left and climbed steadily upwards, passing ancient pockets of habitation, most now long-since empty. It made me wonder who built homes here in the middle of nowhere, and what did they do to make ends meet? It's still a shame to see the disused buildings, but understandable that their upkeep has proved unviable. We fuelled up at the afternoon brew-stop, from where we knew there would be a tough climb to our destination.

We were now in the volcanic region, and in the distance we could see stunning pinnacles and peaks; obviously the steep walls of ancient craters, now lush and green, but with dramatic cliffs stretching upwards. They weren't in the distance for long, and we soon began the climb, steeply at first - probably steeper than anything we'd attempted so far. There was a flatter section in the middle, providing respite before a long and tough ascent to the crater viewpoint at the top. This was the first significant climb of the trip, and I made sure that I took it at my own pace, Bob by my side, with occasional stops if I felt I was starting to breathe too hard. The anticipation was worse than the reality, and I managed fine, soon seeing the 'van rouge' up ahead with Isabelle cheering us on to the top. She wanted to make sure we stopped and didn't miss the viewpoint which was a little off the road. It felt like quite an achievement to get to the top without getting off to push, although it was only a taster of what was to come over the rest of the trip, but we took our selfies and hugged each other, pleased with what we'd done, before setting off for the steep descent into Le Mont Dore and the Grand Hotel.

This was primarily a ski resort, geared up for walkers and climbers in the summertime, but we could tell that its main income came from the winter trade. The imposing hotel was in the centre of town, with chateau-style turrets at its corners, and was a little dated but comfortable. We arranged to meet Vicky and Trevor for drinks, then on to dinner at a local barbeque restaurant. We were now becoming firm friends, and despite only knowing them for a week, Vicky and I often had 'no holds barred' discussions about our saddle issues, much to the dismay of Bob and Trevor! We'd had such a great evening, with lots of laughter, and we felt a nightcap was in order, so hunted for a bar which was still open. We weren't late by UK standards, but in France we had generally struggled to find places open beyond 10pm. Our persistence paid off and we found ourselves in a loud bar, throwing a golf ball for the resident Alsatian dog, and rounding off the evening nicely.

Day 7. Le Mont Dore to St Flour
Miles – 66
Ascent – 5951ft
Average Speed – 9.92mph
Calories – 3870

We hadn't slept well. Our bed was particularly squeaky, and every time either of us moved, it woke the other. This had obviously been quite some hotel in its prime, and the breakfast buffet was an incredible sight with intricate pastries and cakes, the like of which you would expect in a high-end patisserie. But it's just not what I fancied for breakfast, there was little savoury at all, and I found myself yearning for a bacon butty. However, suitably refreshed, we eagerly awaited the morning brief.

Today was billed on the route notes as one of the hardest days of the tour, and there was to be a tough climb out of the town first thing – we were in a ski resort after all, so that should have been a bit of a clue. There was also a significant headwind, and as we left town on the busy road out, climbing steeply, we were battling against the elements which slowed me to a crawl and I was beginning to worry about what lay ahead. Once we turned off the main road onto the lane which leads to the summit of the first col, the gradient eased a little, but we were still climbing steadily, twisting and turning, in and out of the strong wind. It was beautiful scenery, but I could barely turn my head to look, as I was going too slowly and wobbled in the wind if I wasn't concentrating. So I asked Bob to stop a couple of times to take photos of the views, so I could have a look later!

I was breathing hard now, struggling to keep my heart rate under control. I knew I should really stop for a rest, but I wasn't confident I'd get going again in this wind, so pressed onwards, thankful for a flatter section around the next bend. Bob was a little way behind me on this flat part, as he'd stopped for pictures, and so whilst there was some respite from the gradient, I pulled out my water bottle for a much needed slurp. However, to put my bottle back required me to stop pedalling to get it past my knee, and I found that as I stopped pedalling, I wobbled frantically at this slow speed in the strong wind, and so I just couldn't put the bottle away. Having tried a couple of times, I was starting to panic, my heart rate was soaring, my breathing strained, and I was getting lightheaded. By the time Bob had caught up with me, I saw sense and stopped, gasping, dizzy, and a little frightened.

It didn't take too long to recover, but that had been a warning shot to me, to heed the advice from the hospital and to listen to my body. There would be many more climbs on the trip, and much more difficult ones, so I needed to look after myself and stop sooner – walk for a while if I had to. Bob gave me a push start against the wind, and we set off again, plodding slowly upwards side by side. At times he offered me his water bottle so I didn't have to pull out mine, and we made it to the top without needing to stop again, where Isabelle was waiting with some of the others to cheer us up the last stretch. Maybe I would have been fine if it wasn't for the wind, but I made sure I was rested before we set off again.

From there we had a long sweeping descent down the other side of the col, which was the best stretch of road I had ever ridden to date. It was exhilarating! The gradient was gentle, the bends wide, the tarmac smooth as silk, with no kerbs or edges to steal your concentration. The countryside had opened up, and it felt almost Alpine, with chalets tucked into the hillsides, cows clanging their bells in the fields, views for miles, and I felt quite euphoric - grinning like a madwoman as I drifted down absorbing the scene. I was still smiling when Trevor and Vicky flagged us down towards the bottom of the hillside at a café for a very welcome coffee stop, and after that the four of us (with Dylan who was 'sweep' today) rode and chatted up and down the hills in the long stretch between the brew-stop and lunch.

The female anatomy suffers on a bike, no matter how good your saddle and shorts are, and it has already been well documented that Vicky and I were both suffering after so many long consecutive days cycling. It wasn't just soreness around the 'sit bones' (I have more than enough natural padding in this area!), or chafing from constant movement against the seat; there was also discomfort with our 'soft tissue', despite us both having saddles with cut-outs designed to minimise pressure on this area. Being squashed hard into the seat as you crawl up a long hill can cut off the circulation to the soft tissue, leaving you uncomfortably numb, and then you can't tell whether you're causing further damage. It's easily remedied by standing up on the pedals, allowing the blood to flow again. Vicky was stronger than me, and could stand and pedal up some of the sections of hills, but I found that pedalling out of the seat on climbs was more tiring, made me breathless quicker, and I had to wait for the downhills to get out of the saddle. But these longer climbs meant that the relief wasn't coming quickly enough, and we ended up just shouting 'bum break' every now and then, where we would stop to catch our breath and stand up for a while. On one such 'bum break', as Vicky and I eased from our perch, we were both clearly thinking the same thought, but it was me who vocalised it. "It's that sudden rush of blood when you stop – it's not entirely unpleasant!", and we both giggled, blushing hard when we realised that Dylan had caught us up and had clearly heard much more than he wanted to! I'm not sure who was more embarrassed…

Quickly changing the subject, we noticed some cows in the distance which appeared to be loose on the road. We are both very wary of cows, and one of these had fierce-looking horns. Dylan sensed our fear, and rode on ahead with Bob and Trevor, to try to move the cows on. There were three loose cows and they scattered as the blokes approached on their bikes, but were clearly getting agitated – almost as agitated as us girls at the back! They separated, two to one side of the road, and one to the opposite verge, but this spooked them even more, and they were soon running randomly in the road. Vicky and I were nervously keeping a safe distance behind, so that by the time the men had the cows calmer and together in one place, we were able to cycle past as fast as we could, with the three men on their bikes as a barrier between us. Completely irrational, but we had been panicking a bit, and looking back, it was absurd that two grown women should have been so scared!

We had a heavy rain shower to contend with for the last 10 miles to the lunch stop, and were quickly soaked through, with the rain pelting heavily like hailstones on our helmets. When we arrived at the café, most of the other riders had already left, allowing us to spread out, hang up jackets, and relax over lunch. The café had no toilets, but there was a public loo just around the corner. Vicky and I both shied away from public loos normally, most being a hole in the ground, but needs must, and so I headed out there with my pot of Sudocrem, to provide some lubrication for the afternoon's ride. There was no lock on the door, but it was unnecessary anyway, as there was a full-length clear glass window so that anyone approaching could see whether the toilet was occupied or not!

One more climb after lunch was followed by the most amazing 15 mile-long descent, so gradual that you could pop your bike into top gear, and pedal softly down without picking up too much speed. We were heading down the side of a long straight valley, with rolling moorland and flower meadows as our companions. The further down the valley we drifted, the more dramatic the scenery became, with quarries cut out of the sides, and forests growing on the tops. As we whizzed through the town of Allanches, Bob pointed out an enormous graveyard, akin to those you see in Paris, just to the side of the road, and further along we saw a church with 4 enormous bells open to the elements, not hidden beneath a steeple. I was loving this kind of cycling – coasting at speeds I'd never dream of riding in the UK, looking more at what's around me than at the road, but brimming with elation and the widest of smiles.

At the afternoon brew-stop, we chatted with Isabelle whilst watching the dark clouds brewing, and feeling the humidity rising. The best idea was to press on as quickly as we could as this storm looked menacing, so we headed out up the first of two climbs that lay between us and our destination. This first stretch was on a busy road, and cars were passing us quickly as we listened to the thunder rolling in from the distance, wondering when the deluge would hit us. Thankfully, by the time the worst of it arrived, we spotted a picnic area to the side of the road, where the four of us sheltered under trees (not the best idea in a storm, but there was no other option!) waiting for the thunder, lightning and heavy rain to pass, trying to make light of a bad situation by convincing ourselves that things couldn't get any worse. When we left our little comfort zone, and ventured out into the now-lighter drizzle, we could see St Flour in the distance, perched on a hilltop, shrouded in mist. This would normally have been picturesque, but today it just signified one more climb - and more rain!

We pushed on as fast as our weary legs could go, to try to get there and get dried, but the climb up to the town was steep, and my energy was fading fast. What's more, from out of nowhere, the traffic became suddenly busy, the roadworks were confusing to navigate, the Garmins were too wet to read properly, and we somehow all missed the turn to our accommodation. However, the Peak Tours team were already becoming concerned, as Dylan had arrived as sweep before us, (he must have sailed past when we were sheltering from the storm) and in these conditions they were worried that something was wrong. Isabelle and Alberto had moved both van rouges to strategic points, and they'd begun phoning all our mobiles - which we were ignoring, not wanting to stop in the rain to answer our phones. As we were about to head steeply down the hill out of town, I spotted the van, shouted ahead to Bob to stop him disappearing off, and we all did a U-turn. It was a steep push up a soaking cobbled alleyway to the old monastery where we were staying, but Isabelle was clearly relieved to have all her chickens safely home to roost.

The monastery was massive – ancient and quirky, and in a beautiful setting, and on any other day we would have been pleased to spend the night there. However, tonight we were wet, tired and miserable, and we longed for a good shower, and somewhere to dry our sodden kit. The rooms had been the monks cells (well, they felt like cells!), which had now been updated slightly to en-suite - after a fashion. There was no heating, and so no way of drying clothes and shoes ready for tomorrow. Later, dodging the incessant rain, we met in town with Vicky and Trevor to whinge about the weather over drinks and pizza, and the trials of the day began to melt away with each passing glass… A difficult and eventful day.

Day 8. St Flour to Mende
Miles – 52 (I did 46!)
Ascent – 4992ft
Average Speed – 9.77mph
Calories – 2778

The monastery - indeed the whole town - was in cloud when we woke, but it lifted slowly so that by the morning briefing, we could almost see half a mile ahead! The route notes suggested that today would be 'up and down' all day, which is Peak Tours speak for fairly hilly, with some climbs longer and harder than others. The day began with a long descent to a lake at the bottom of a valley where there stood an amazing viaduct, built by Eiffel of tower fame, spanning the deep gorge. It clearly had Eiffel's style written all over it, and was resplendent in its red paint against a backdrop of the dramatic limestone gorge. Skirting around the edge of the lake beneath the bridge, we could see the mirrored image of the surrounding hillsides reflected in the water's surface, in that lovely peaceful stillness which often descends after a storm has passed. But what goes down, must come up, and we were soon climbing steeply up the side of the gorge to the brew-stop in a little village nestling above the patchy low cloud.

We were on top of a plateau now, and the road rose and fell gently with lovely views on either side. We felt like we were really high up, looking down on the flat rolling fields below, but we could still hear thunder in the distance. Bob and I were cycling alone again today, with Alberto following closely behind. Towards lunchtime, we approached Saint-Chély-d'Apcher, a town twinned with Tadcaster, and which was obviously quite a large commercial centre. The outskirts became busy with traffic, industrial estates and apartment blocks, and Alberto took the lead, to help us navigate through the unfamiliar territory. Threading down the steep main street in the centre of town was a real surprise – quaint cobbled roads and narrow lanes with bustling shops either side, and a steady stream of cars waiting their turn for the parking spaces. This would have been a nice place to stop and explore, but we needed to press on, so we followed Alberto down, over wet cobbles and slippery manhole covers - sometimes on the pavement - until we were out at the far side of town, and paralleling a motorway to the next town along. This was not my favourite stretch of road, pedalling with the constant thrum of heavy traffic noise, and I was more than ready for the lunch break.

As we entered the café, a group of the faster cyclists were just getting ready to leave, so there were plenty of places to sit, eat and rest. Within minutes of the first wave leaving, the skies darkened ominously, and we watched as the lightning flashes got closer and closer. A thunderstorm of biblical proportions hit, with torrential rain and hailstones slamming deafeningly onto the Perspex roof of the café, whilst we sat sipping coffee and feeling sorry for those who had already set off. It was truly horrendous weather, and there was no point in leaving until it had blown through, because debris and water would still be rushing down the roads in its wake.

There were two significant climbs left today, followed by a steep six mile descent to our destination. As we set off with Vicky and Trevor, Alberto took a few calls from Isabelle, warning him that the group at the front had been caught in the hailstorm, and that the roads higher up were treacherous. There had been little shelter to be found by the riders ahead, so they had soldiered on in the terrible conditions. However, at the top of the second climb the hailstones were huge, and had left a layer of thick slush on the roads, through which they couldn't ride. For safety, they had to push for a while, paddling through the soft ice up and over the summit, until they reached the point where it was thawing quickly on the lower sections. But a few of the riders got incredibly cold, and it must have been very unpleasant.

Isabelle had abandoned the brew-stop and was acting as safety vehicle, offering to give lifts to anyone who didn't want to ride through this - although no-one had yet taken up her offer. By the time we arrived at the second climb, the weather had improved dramatically, and the icy layer was melting fast. We could easily ride slowly upwards in the black lines left in the slush by passing vehicles, and there was a cold mist rising eerily from the road surface, chilling our legs. Vicky and I were a little spooked by the reports coming back from the others about their difficult descent on the other side – it was one thing to be climbing slowly through the slush, but an entirely different matter to be speeding downwards in it. Isabelle's van was parked temptingly just before the summit, and so we made the sensible decision to stop and accept a lift for the six mile descent. With our parting words to Bob and Trevor to be extra careful, knowing that their freedom from us would coax them to ride fast, we both jumped in the van and headed downwards. Had we known that within a mile the sun had cleared the road completely, we would have persevered, but hindsight is a wonderful thing, and we chose the safe option.

Mende was a lovely town, with a majestic cathedral at its heart, occupied by a local wedding party as we arrived. By now the sun was beating down, and we all gathered in the town square for pre-dinner drinks. Bob and I chose to eat alone that evening, and picked a lovely little restaurant off the beaten track, which was really busy with locals, and served traditional French food with a modern twist. A lovely end to another eventful day!

Day 9. Mende to Vallon Pont D'Arc
Miles – 74
Ascent – 6117ft
Average Speed – 12.22mph
Calories – 3776

We woke to what felt like a different season, with glorious blue skies and already feeling warm before morning briefing. Today the roads would be generally busier and wider than we'd encountered so far on the trip, but it was all still relative, and tourist traps aside, we didn't notice the traffic. The morning saw a very gentle climb for around 15 miles, but so gradual that I didn't feel the need for any 'bum breaks'.

We were following the River Lot upstream along steep sided valleys lush with forest and gorse. We passed through hamlets and villages whose houses and churches appeared to be built from the limestone rocks hewn from the cliffs on either side, probably when they were cutting a passage for the road. As we reached the head of this valley, the views opened out into a mountain vista, with nothing but blue skies and rugged hills to be seen. We passed a sign declaring the border between Atlantic France and Mediterranean France, and it felt as though someone had flicked a switch – a complete contrast to the views we'd had over the last couple of days. I don't know how, but it just felt 'Mediterranean'. Where yesterday we'd seen worms and snails in the road, today there were lizards darting before your wheels, and we could smell pine, gorse and hot tarmac.

Slowly sauntering down the other side of the hill, I found I kept welling up. We were on a lovely 15 mile-long descent, and it felt like this was what I'd waited five years for. Bob and I side-by-side, barely pedalling, but whizzing gently down smooth roads, passing by villages nestled into the hillsides with churches or what looked like old monasteries, and the occasional beautiful chateau in the middle of nowhere. We stopped a couple of times for pictures, but mostly just enjoyed ourselves, taking in the views with smiles for miles, and I kept muttering "wow" beneath my breath. Dylan was with us for the majority of this section, and he was clearly proud of the beauty of his country - I think he was enjoying the emotional rush along with us.

After a picnic lunch in the sunshine for a change, we had quite a severe descent for a few miles where we were heading down to the Ardeche river valley. This downhill section was hard for me, and I had a few stops to rest my hands from pulling the brakes. But the scenery when I could look up was stunning – terracotta-roofed houses, cherry sellers at the roadside and cracked white earth. Once in the Ardeche valley, there were vineyards as far as the eye could see, the beautiful blue/green river snaking its way along the base, campsites offering canoes for hire, and the hills seemed far, far away.

We had over 20 miles to cover along the valley floor, but it was hot, very hot, and the heat reflecting from the tarmac made sure we were evenly baked from all angles. Although the gradients were gentle this afternoon, the busier tourist traffic and coaches meant we had to concentrate hard on staying safe in the hot wake as they sped by, and I was feeling more than a little jaded. There had been no shelter from the sun for what seemed like an age and I pressed on hard, just wanting to get the miles done. But the heat and speed combined to tire me quickly and Bob and I stopped briefly in the shade of a roadside building, to finish off our now-warm water bottles. We shouldn't grumble about the sunshine after the last few days, but this felt dangerously hot.

Isabelle as usual was on hand just round the corner at an unscheduled extra stop to fill us up with cold water and put cold compresses on the back of our necks, which was lovely, and I felt I could have stayed there and let her look after me all afternoon. However, we had to pedal onwards through the heat and the traffic, and as we neared our destination, an amazing sight came into view: the Pont d'Arc - a natural stone archway, huge and magnificent, through which the lazy Ardeche flowed silently. The scenery was so beautiful, so magical, that all my woes faded. We stopped to take it all in, blocking out the hordes of cars and coaches all trying to pull in to do the same. It really was gorgeous – the green water against the steep valley sides, and a stream of canoes gently paddling beneath the archway, watched by lines of spectators on the walking trails on either side. And the best news was that our finish point for the day was less than a half mile away!

The hotel was wonderful, our bedroom had a shaded balcony for my post-ride beer, and later we all ate together outside on the terrace. It was a very special evening, with much laughter, and wonderfully soft cushions on the seats.

Towards the end of the night, those of us left having a nightcap or two were discussing with Isabelle the inevitable Mont Ventoux ascent which was looming on day 11. This is the Holy Grail to many cyclists, a climb which features often on the Tour De France, and Peak Tours include it on their route, offering an alternative for those who choose not to do this notoriously difficult climb. I had said all along that I was here to do the End-to-End, and didn't need the extra hill in the middle. I had intended to thoroughly enjoy my French experience, and climbing Ventoux was something I knew I wouldn't find a whole lot of fun. Bob was quite happy to be with me, whichever route I opted for, and so the choice was entirely mine. Given the hospital advice, and my little 'episode' a couple of days ago, I was certain I would plump for the alternative, but there was that niggling feeling that I might be the only one who didn't attempt the climb, and that maybe I'd regret it. After all, I was pretty fit now, had lots of climbing under my belt and had mostly managed to do the ascents without any after effects. But I didn't have to decide yet, and there was another amazing day ahead tomorrow.

Day 10. Vallon Pont D'Arc to Vaison-la-Romaine
Miles – 58
Ascent – 5444ft
Average Speed – 10.65mph
Calories – 3189

We had the most beautiful view for breakfast, our hotel snuggled into the limestone gorge, but it was already 21° as we waited for our morning briefing, being dive-bombed by beautiful yellow/white moths. This was to be a tough morning of climbs and descents, followed by an easier afternoon, with just one big hill late on. We set off in sunglasses and sunscreen, and had to ascend almost immediately from the valley floor to the top of the Ardeche gorge. This was indeed a difficult climb, and I made sure to have a few 'bum breaks' which doubled as a chance to catch my breath. But the scenery on the way up was simply stunning, and we used the breaks to take in the views.

Once we reached the top of the climb, the road followed the crest of the Ardeche gorge, undulating along the ridge, occasionally through wooded areas where goats roamed freely in the bushes, their bells tinkling peacefully, and at other times bare rock flanked the road. There were thousands of hairy caterpillars crawling across the road, presumably they turn into the moths which fluttered with us at breakfast, but there must have been thousands more squashed into orange dots on the tarmac. Every now and then, there was a signpost warning of a viewpoint ahead, and they meant it! We pulled in at almost every 'balcon' to take in the sheer size of this natural wonder, take photos, and just marvel at the green water below, amazed that such a gentle stream could carve such a vast and deep gorge.

It is difficult to describe what we were seeing – the likes of which I'd never seen before; a steep sided valley with exposed layered rock on the upper slopes, and lush green vegetation lower down towards the vivid green water. The scale of it was immense: we were very high up, the 'stream' was actually really wide, and you could clearly see that the dots in the distance were in fact canoes, paddling downstream. The river meandered gently at times, almost looping in parts, and then sometimes was straight as an arrow, and we could imagine how awe-inspiring it must be to observe this from a canoe down below. Surely in the winter time, they must offer white-water rafting, as the river bed looked like it would be very impressive in full flow. We were looking down on the birds of prey which were enjoying soaring in the thermals, and it genuinely felt like a privilege to be here, absorbing these scenes.

As we neared the head of the gorge, someone pointed out in the distance the summit of Mont Ventoux, with its distinctive bare white summit and tower on top. It looked so far away, that I could barely believe that tomorrow would see us all climbing it, or cycling round. Surely we wouldn't get close enough to it in one day on a bicycle?

Our time on the crest of this jaw-dropping gorge was done, and we had a long sweeping descent down to the valley floor beyond. Here again were campsites and canoes for hire, and as we crossed the Ardeche for the last time, we were in Côtes Du Rhône country, with its vast vineyards on the flat hot plains. Here we saw winery tours and tastings on offer, and there's obviously a Côtes Du Rhône route which would take in several of these tours - best done with a duty driver in tow, and definitely not on a bicycle! Our route crossed the Rhône twice, before ending up on a traffic-free cycle path for a few miles, until we stopped for lunch at a cool shady picnic area.

It was now steaming hot, and again we had a lot of miles to cover across fairly flat land, with just one short sharp climb half way, but with little or no shelter from the sun. It was best to do as we did yesterday, and press on as hard and fast as I could manage, keeping our heads up to take in the scenery, but not stopping for photos in the heat. All the while we could see Mont Ventoux looming larger as we drew nearer, and although it looked an enormous hill, its slopes looked gradual, not too steep. Around four miles from our hotel, there was a small village square with a fountain under a huge tree, where several of our group had stopped and were enjoying the shade with cold drinks and ice creams. We spent a very pleasant half hour or so beneath the trees, Vicky dipping her feet in the fountain, Alberto dipping his dreadlocks, and the rest of us chatting and laughing as if we were on holiday!

Before dinner, Isabelle called us all to a briefing about the Ventoux climb the next day. Safety was obviously paramount in her mind. Several of our group had done this tour before, and were keen to improve on their Ventoux times. Others wanted to see how fast they could climb it, but the majority wanted simply to make it to the top. Isabelle and her team had to cater for everyone's needs, and use the two 'van rouges' to provide the best support for everyone – there would be no support for anyone who chose to take the alternative route. This is clearly a tried and tested formula, with the two vans leap-frogging each other to various points to provide water and refreshments for those who wanted to stop for a break, but also to top up water bottles on the go for those who were trying to climb it in one. She explained how the day would run, and once she was happy that everyone was comfortable, she asked was anyone choosing the alternative route.......

I had spent all day battling with my decision. I had studied the elevation profile, spoken to those who had climbed it before, and I knew that the gradients weren't as severe as some of the short hills Bob and I had conquered during our training runs. But it was a 14 mile long climb in the heat with no respite, and although my legs still felt fairly fit and strong, they had cycled over 700 miles since we left Ouistreham. By now I also knew I would be the only one of our group to opt out. Bob was leaving the decision to me, but if I chose Ventoux, he made me promise that I would listen to my body, and not push too hard, getting off to walk or getting in the van with Isabelle if I felt I needed to. No shame in that, given the circumstances. For five years I had looked forward to this trip, and for five years I had vowed that I wanted the End-to-End, not Mont Ventoux. But now my End-to-End was 23 miles short, thanks to a broken spoke and some hailstones, so maybe... just maybe?

……..I stayed silent, no-one raised their hand, and the briefing was over. Isabelle came straight to me, took me to one side by the arm and asked was I doing this for me, or for peer pressure. I didn't really have a truthful answer, and for some bizarre reason, my bottom lip began to wobble – I guess I still wasn't really convinced I should try the climb. I'm not sure whether I'd mentioned my doctor's advice to her before now, but she sensed that there was something wrong, and said that she'd be there for me if I needed to bail out, that my health was the most important thing, not some bloody mountain!

Our hotel was on the far edge of an old medieval city, with amazing architecture and a few tourist shops and restaurants. We were all keen to get an early night rather than explore the town, so we plumped for the nearest restaurant, and we ate with the others before taking a bottle of cold local wine back to the hotel to slurp on the terrace with our usual drinking buddies, overlooking the valley below in the sunset. It was a truly beautiful place - the perfect end to a lovely evening, and we slept well.

Day 11. Vaison La Romaine to Sault
Miles – 38
Ascent – 7219ft
Average Speed – 7.87mph
Calories – 2888

We were to set off earlier today. I assume to get the climb done before the worst heat of the day, and also to make sure we finished early and got plenty of rest before a long day in the saddle tomorrow. Breakfast was lovely in the hotel, which is clearly a cyclist's haunt, with memorabilia and old maps of the Tour De France covering the walls.

The first 10 miles were undulating, with short but sharper climbs and falls, towards the town of Malaucene, where Isabelle was waiting to make sure everyone had what they needed before the main climb. We had passed through some lovely little private vineyards and olive groves, over ancient stone bridges, and our legs had definitely warmed up in readiness for the 'big one'.

Malaucene was the official start point, and so it began…

The route was forested at first, providing good shelter from the increasing power of the sun, and it was already pretty warm. This was a wide and good surfaced road, with two lanes for motor vehicles, and a cycle lane painted at each side. As this was the Mecca for cyclists, there was an awful lot of folk doing exactly the same as us, some alone, some in groups, but the traffic was generally courteous, and we could concentrate on our own mission. We were passed by numerous bikes of different descriptions, including more than a handful of electric

107

bikes, but it was interesting to see the types of people who were attempting this challenge, and most shouted encouragement as they overtook.

There were marker posts at each kilometre, stating how far to the summit, and what the average gradient was for the next Km - the first marker we noticed was 20Km to go. The gradient was manageable for the first four miles or so, and I was happy plodding along, able to chat to Bob as he pedalled slowly behind me. We had to stop for occasional 'bum breaks' and also to drink, as we were moving too slowly for me to grab my bottle on the move, but we progressed upwards round the hairpins and zig-zags comfortably to the first brew-stop. I was feeling quite confident that if things remained the same, I would be slow, but absolutely fine.

We set off again, obviously at the back of the pack, with Dylan the 'sweep' keeping a discreet distance behind us. The road here was less sheltered from the sun and the heat built quickly, but I could take my mind off things by expressing my disgust at how fast some of the cyclists were whizzing down from the summit on the other side of the road. I sounded like my mother, with 'it'll end in tears!', and 'that's just reckless!', but it provided a good distraction.

There were longer stretches here in between hairpins, and some helpful soul had chalked on the road the actual gradient, so instead of thinking that the kilometre I was pedalling had an average of 11%, I could clearly read that the next 100 metres was 14%, the next 13% etc, and somehow that made things worse. After a few bum breaks and around three miles since the brew-stop, there was a long stretch that alternated between 12% and 14%, with no flatter sections. I plodded on but soon started struggling for breath, feeling lightheaded, and so stopped to rest. Dylan caught us up quickly, and offered me energy bars and water, but it wasn't energy I needed, it was air!

The gradient was too steep, and my legs too wobbly for me to set off on my own, so Bob gave me a push start, and I again plodded upwards for a few hundred metres. But I hadn't really recovered properly, and my breathing was soon hurting, my heart-rate out of control, and I was in danger of passing out. I had to stop, get off, sit down, but my mind was spinning about how ridiculous it was that I couldn't do this, whilst everyone else seemed to be sailing past with no real difficulty. The disappointment, frustration and fatigue welled up inside, leaving my eyes watery and a lump closing my throat, making my breathing even harder. As Bob gave me a big hug to calm me down, Dylan arrived, looking quite alarmed at the state of me, and immediately apologised, assuming it was his fault for somehow pushing me to go faster, because he was behind us! After choking back the tears and a few minutes rest, I decided that enough was enough, and I would walk until the gradient eased a little, but even walking was tough going, and I had to take it slowly.

It was then that I noticed a number of cyclists ahead who were also pushing. Okay, they weren't with our party and looked like older blokes, but it wasn't just me after all, and this gave me a boost. We must have walked around 400m in the end, Bob and Dylan chatting behind, and me battling with my own thoughts just in front, but then the gradient dropped enough for me to want to try to cycle again, and thankfully, after another push start, we saw the 'van rouge' around the next bend. I only had to pedal 200m before I could have another rest!

I sat in a deck chair, drinking sugary drinks and absorbing biscuits until I was ready, and then set off with yet another push up the hill. The gradient eased after a mile or so, and from then it was manageable, with occasional bum breaks and water stops. I hadn't been lifting my head much to take in my surroundings, but quite suddenly we were above the tree line, and the top of the mountain was glaring in the sunshine; its distinctive barren, chalk slopes, and zig-zag road clearly visible all the way to the summit. The hairpins were tight now, and naturally the gradient increased around them, but with the end literally in sight, I pressed on upwards, breathing hard. We knew we were nearing the top when there were photographers snapping your every turn of the pedal, and giving you a push as they popped a note into your jersey pocket. Obviously, if I wanted to, I could have a souvenir photo of me looking sweaty, bedraggled and red-faced, with Bob and Dylan cruising in the background!

The last short stretch was much nicer. About 50m from the top, we could see Isabelle and the red van, along with a good sized group of our party, all clapping, shouting and cheering us on. We had to cycle past them to reach the summit, but with their encouragement ringing in my ears, I knew I'd made it. Bob and I hugged at the summit post, had the obligatory photos, and then took stock of what we'd just done. Alright, it wasn't easy, or pretty, and I can't honestly say I enjoyed it, but I'd made it up Mont Ventoux under my own steam! Bob was just pleased I was in one piece…

The others who were still there came over to give us hugs and congratulations. It turned out we were about 30 minutes later than the last of the other Peak Tours riders, so it was lovely of them to have waited around to see us in. Especially the 'King of the Mountain', who had a staggering 90 minute wait, but who was determined to watch us all finish - a true gentleman. It was cold on the top, so they all quickly began the steep descent to lunch, while Bob and I talked to Isabelle, and put coats on for the journey down. She gave me a huge hug, and looked genuinely relieved that all her riders had made it safely up the mountain. It must be quite a responsibility to have to account for 26 cyclists on such a tough day.

The descent from the summit began quite steeply, a mirror image of what we'd just climbed, down barren switchbacks with tight hairpins. I wasn't feeling great - quite drained and shaky, and more than a little nervous that the trip down the mountain looked like it might be just as hair-raising as the journey up. There was a restaurant a few miles down, where we recharged our batteries properly. I still felt a little light-headed and it took a while for the pizza, fizzy drinks and strong coffee to kick in. I had visions of those cyclists whizzing down at great speed, and it did cross my mind that maybe I should ask Isabelle for a lift, as I would need all the energy I could muster to concentrate on this next descent, and energy was something I was running out of rapidly. But we set off as soon as I was ready, knowing that Isabelle would pass us in the van within the first couple of miles, and I could always flag her down if I wasn't happy. However, the gradient from the restaurant was much kinder, we only needed to brake hard for the corners, and I even began to lift my head and enjoy it. As we sailed down, there was still a steady stream of cyclists panting upwards, and I bet they weren't thinking *I* was travelling too fast!

We were now in lavender country, and as we approached our endpoint, there were fields upon fields of neatly planted rows of this fragrant crop, smelling delicious as we drifted past. Unfortunately, we were about a fortnight too early to see it in full bloom, but we could imagine what a magnificent sight it must be. And we could see the town of Sault in the distance, perched picturesquely on a hillside, and that could only mean one thing - another climb before the finish! It was a very short (but very sharp) climb, and by the time we arrived at our hotel I was shattered, and opted to miss the first of the post-ride beers. Maybe I'd overdone it today…

Once everyone was refreshed we had a lovely evening all together in the courtyard restaurant outside the hotel. They had made us a 'Mont Ventoux' cake, which the King of the Mountain had the privilege of cutting, and we sat with a nightcap or three with Trevor and Vicky, discussing backsides and other issues, with the trials of the day fading quickly. They were very good company, and I was especially pleased to have Vicky around – it felt like we'd known them for years. For the first time today, I began to feel rightly proud that I'd attempted (and managed – almost!) the climb - and more than thankful that Bob had stayed with me all the way.

Day 12. Sault to Moustier-Ste-Marie

Miles – 70

Ascent – 4629ft

Average Speed – 11.61mph

Calories – 3823

I woke Bob early, wrongly thinking we had an earlier start, so we spent half an hour wandering around the town, which was setting up for market day. The stalls were typically French, with beautiful vegetables laid out immaculately, butchers selling horse meat, and lots and lots of lavender for sale. There was a lovely terrace at one end of town, from where the views in the early morning light were stunning. We couldn't believe how far away the summit of Ventoux looked - it's remarkable how much distance we were covering each day.

But everyone has their 'off' day, and this would definitely be mine. Even sauntering around town this morning left me breathing heavily, and I was suffering from pains in my chest. It felt muscular, almost as if I had strained the muscles in my ribs when I was gasping so hard on the climb yesterday. And to top it off, I received a text from the hospital detailing my next tests, which were due a couple of days after we returned from France. I think all this was playing on my mind from the outset today...

After our morning briefing in the medieval square outside the hotel, we set off - along undulating roads through the lavender fields, with the ever-present poppies standing proudly at their edge. The poppies here seemed to have smaller flowers, but were much brighter in colour, and the contrast against the slightly purpling lavender was truly beautiful. It was already stiflingly hot, so we didn't stop to take photos, but just took it all in as we sailed by. It was quite amusing to see a coach full of Oriental tourists parked in a lay-by in the middle of nowhere. The occupants were spilling into the fields, dressed in their Sunday best with parasols, and having their photos taken in amongst the rows of young lavender.

After the first brew-stop, there was a long gentle descent, which was a welcome break for the legs after yesterday, and Trevor and Vicky flagged us down as we approached a pretty market town, suggesting we stop at a café for a cold drink and to use their facilities – we knew we were having a picnic lunch again today, so nice loo's were very welcome! It was a busy little town, and above the row of shops on the steep cobbled main street, there were white walls and gaily painted shutters – we really felt like we were nearing the Mediterranean now.

The picnic lunch was the best yet, with Dylan preparing delicious fresh salads, and I could happily have stayed there in the shade all afternoon, but today was a high mileage day, and we needed to press on. The heat was intense, and I was still finding it uncomfortable to breathe hard. I was over-thinking what was happening in my chest, and I couldn't switch off and just look at the scenery around me. Vicky was feeling the heat too, and the four of us, with Alberto at the back, rode together along the undulations, keeping each other motivated, still passing lavender fields, but now with mountains off to our left in the distance - perhaps the start of the Alps, as they were still snow-capped.

There was one sharp climb this afternoon, and Alberto kindly offered to push Vicky and I in turns, to give us a little helping hand. It was how I imagine an e-bike would work –

114

we would still cycle, but it was much less effort with Alberto pedalling hard beside us, one hand gently on our back, boosting our progress. No matter what, it helped a treat, and we were soon at the top, ready for the sweeping descent. We were now riding through woodland with old, gnarled pine trees and bright yellow gorse in full bloom, its distinctive aroma clinging in the air as we drifted downwards.

This afternoon saw a steady incline for the last 12 miles or so, but the gradient was so gentle that it almost looked flat to the eye - but to the legs, it felt anything but flat! The heat, tired legs, and straighter roads left many of our cyclists describing this stretch as though riding through treacle. Nearing the end of the day, we could see Moustier in the distance, suspended on the cliff side, which meant yet another climb to the hotel. I slowed to a snail's pace, and Alberto gave me another push to get me the last mile to home - my hero!

The hotel was great, with a huge room, but no air-con, and I flopped on the bed while Bob had a shower. Throughout the day, I had come to the decision that I would miss the next morning's climb, billed as being the second toughest of the trip. I hadn't felt strong all day, and it was playing on my mind that maybe I had pushed too hard on Ventoux. I had already missed out on the End-to-End, so missing the first 11 miles of climb the next day wouldn't make much of a difference. I had heard that the Verdon gorge (which we'd cycle tomorrow) was the most spectacular day of the tour, and having thoroughly loved the Ardeche gorge, I wanted to feel well enough to enjoy this one too.

The only problem was that admitting it to everyone, and asking for a lift in the van, felt like a failure and a tad embarrassing. Bob knew it was the right decision for me, and I think he was relieved that I was being sensible for once. I don't really understand why I felt embarrassed – this was meant to be a holiday after all - but I did, and that evening, we discussed it over pre-dinner drinks with our new 'best friends'. It turned out that Vicky was also considering a lift up the hill tomorrow, but for saddle reasons, rather than health…

We put it to the back of our minds, exploring the beautiful old town, with its waterfalls running through the centre, and ancient churches and buildings built into the hillside, some on stone 'stilts' - an amazing feat of engineering even by today's standards. There was a golden star suspended on chains between two cliffs high above the town, glinting brightly in the evening sunshine, and it was a very peaceful spot. We looked for a restaurant based on the comfort of the seats rather than the menu (!), and plumped for a lovely little place, built in the cloisters of an old church, which served good food in a cool, quirky room with a vaulted ceiling - and lovely deep cushions…

Afterwards, for our traditional nightcap, we headed back to the bar opposite the hotel, and found Isabelle talking to a few of the others. Vicky confessed to her that she was thinking about missing the first hill, but I knew that by morning, she'd change her mind and jump on her bike. There was much 'bottom' banter, and it was great to end the evening with such laughter. When the others had gone I sat with Isabelle, explaining how I had struggled with my chest today, that it might well all be in my mind, but that I felt I ought to miss the hill in the morning. But I also confessed that I was embarrassed to be doing so. Professional and caring as ever, she had a plan, and assured me that she would be discreet. Disappointed in myself, but knowing I'd made the right choice, Bob and I retired to a very good night's sleep.

Day 13. Moustier-St-Marie to Castellane
Miles - 50 (I did 39!)
Ascent – 4712ft
Average Speed – 10.5mph
Calories – 2212

It was another beautiful morning, and at the briefing I stood with my head bowed, feeling mixed emotions. As the others set off up the hill, Vicky gave me a hug, and said she'd see me at the top, before delicately easing herself into the saddle for the climb. To spare my blushes, Isabelle had wanted everyone to leave, before loading me and my bike into the van, and Bob set off last to catch up with the others.

It would be an 11.5 mile journey to the brew-stop just before the top of the col, where I'd jump on my bike as if nothing had happened. But those 11.5 miles were wonderful! Isabelle and I reminisced about our area of Manchester, and it turns out that we have much common ground in that neck of the woods. We talked about family, and I explained why I'd cancelled my trip last year after Mum and Dad fell ill. When I told her how comforting it was for the family to have given them a joint funeral, I swear I saw tears in her eyes and she held my hand. Isabelle is lovely and such easy company - I wish she still lived in Manchester, as I'm confident that she and I would become close, given the opportunity.

We drove up the gorge along the route of the cyclists, and she stopped at all the viewpoints, as I would have done, so I could get the same experience and photos as the others, but without sweating and breathing too hard! From my comfortable seat, I knew I'd made the right choice. The hill was shorter than Ventoux, looked steeper in parts, and some of the hairpins were really tight, but the higher we drove, the happier I was that I had wimped out, and I no longer cared who knew - I wouldn't have enjoyed this climb. When we reached the brew-stop, Isabelle clicked into motion, setting out the drinks and refreshments. I was clearly in the way, so I walked over to the viewpoint, taking in the scenery, waiting for the others to arrive.

I'm not sure how I can describe the Verdon Gorge. Neither words nor photos can do it justice, and I'm not confident my vocabulary is adequate either. But I stood, taking it all in, with my eyes misting, and my breath firmly stolen. At 25Km long, and up to 700 metres deep, the gorge is simply stunning – a natural beauty beyond comprehension, and second only in size to the Grand Canyon.

Our relationship with it had begun before the climb, where the bright azure blue waters empty into Lac de Saint Croix as they emerge from the limestone cliffs. The colour of the river, and the peacefulness of the lake as it opens into lush rolling countryside, gave no hint of the journey the water had made to reach this point. Once on the climb, the viewpoints offered glimpses of deep, deep ravines - horizontal layers of limestone revealed over thousands of years as the water carved its path through the mountains. The river looked narrow at times, with the steep sides gouged out vertically, and at other points the valley floor was wider, and the shallower sides suggested the flow rate here was more gentle. Where the valley opened up, I could see caves in the rocks partway up the cliffs, presumably evidence of when the river flowed at that level, and clawed out the hollows as it raced by. Some of the slopes were covered in greenery, whilst others were so dramatically steep, that nothing would ever cling long enough to grow, and all the while I could see the road on the opposite side of the gorge, snaking its way up and along the crest, presumably as we were about to.

At the brew-stop viewpoint the gorge was vast, allowing the eye to take in the enormity of this magical place. The river was still the brightest of blue, but so far below us, that it was difficult to believe that such a tiny ribbon of a stream could leave such a majestic mark on its surroundings. It was truly memorable to be there, and I know I will return one day. In the distance, I could see the chalky peak of Mont Ventoux, and I once again marvelled at the fact that just two days ago, we stood at the top.

Before I could dry my eyes, the first of the cyclists were arriving at the brew-stop. Bob, who had set off last from the hotel, arrived in fourth, having enjoyed climbing the hill at his own pace for once! Once he caught his breath, we cycled together the last mile of the climb, which was still significant, but with my fresh legs, it didn't pose a problem. The road then undulated along the crest of the gorge, sometimes steeply, but with several 'balcons' allowing us to stop and take in the sights all around us. The heat was stifling, but the view stops were frequent and so magnificent, that it went largely unnoticed, until we hit another short sharp climb just before lunch. Bob and I were at the back again by now, and the others were sitting outside the restaurant in the shade, awaiting our arrival with cheers and applause - I was starting to feel like a rock-star, or were they simply glad we'd arrived, as it meant they could start their lunch?

Suitably refreshed, we continued along the gorge to its head, and crossed a small bridge where the scenery changed again, becoming heavily forested, with piles of newly sawn pine at the road edge, attacking our senses with that Christmas-Tree scent. The traffic had been busy along the climb up the col, mostly motorbikes, but now we were again the only travellers along this stretch, and to our left, we could see the most amazing hills. This was stratification, I was reliably informed, and showed layers of rock, sometimes angled, sometimes near-vertical, which over thousands of years had been pushed and squeezed into place as the earth's crust moved beneath. It was a live geology lesson right before our eyes.

As we dropped down to the valley bottom, to follow the River Verdon upstream for the afternoon, our lesson in rock formations had only just begun. Around every bend, and with every turn of the head, there was something to make us shout 'Wow'! The crystal blue waters to one side, close enough to almost touch, the stripes and layers in the rocks all around us, the tunnels and overhangs of rock under which the road passed, all meant that this was by far the best days cycling Bob and I had ever had. We pedalled slowly, trying to make it last forever, smiling, emotional, and stopping often, sometimes to take photos, but mostly just to enjoy our surroundings, vowing that we'd return here someday.

But all good things do have to end - in the distance we could see a church perched high on a rock, which looked as though only Rapunzel's prince would be able to gain access. This was the Chapel Notre-Dame-du-Roc, which stands proudly above the pretty town of Castellane, our destination for tonight.

After a quick turnaround, our usual 'gang of four' headed to a bar, planning on treating ourselves to real French champagne. We deserved to celebrate, but thought that buying champagne in Nice tomorrow might prove expensive, so why not enjoy a glass now after such an amazing day! Unbelievably, nowhere seemed to stock champagne, just prosecco, which was a poor substitute but we drank it nonetheless. We then looked for a restaurant we'd found online, which turned out to be a hidden gem; small, less touristy, with excellent food, and for once, we didn't bother with a nightcap before retiring. It had been a very good day.

Day 14. Castellane to Nice
Miles – 57
Ascent – 4176ft
Average Speed – 11.7mph
Calories – 2866

Vicky and Trevor had been woken at 5.30am by the strangest of sights - goat and sheep herders driving their animals through the streets of the town, banging drums to keep them all moving! Thankfully, Bob and I slept through this, and enjoyed a lovely breakfast, with pancakes and maple syrup providing a much-needed break from the usual continental fare.

There was a carnival atmosphere at the morning briefing, with all of us in our matching Peak Tours jerseys, and smiles from ear to ear. Although we didn't want our adventure to end,

I think we were all ready for going home now, and today would see us completing our coast-to-coast. It was a little cooler, with a hazy covering of cloud which would soon burn away.

The morning saw the last of our climbs, one final col before cycling along a plateau to the lunch stop. The scenery was still beautiful but nothing could top yesterday, and I was finding the hills tough going again. We were soon at the back with the sweep, and Alberto gave me a push, telling me to just ask whenever I wanted his help. The plateau top was equally challenging. Wide expanses of land with no shade, no interesting features, just meadows left to grow wild, with poppies and other wildflowers in abundance. There was a headwind and a slight incline, which made this stretch feel much tougher than the elevation profile had suggested, and it was a slog.

Isabelle clearly wanted everyone to cycle closer together today, to make sure we didn't arrive at the end point too spread out. A few miles before lunch, she had stopped the others at a viewpoint at the end of the climb, so Bob and I had our traditional cheers and applause as we turned up. Then we all set off again down a short but steep descent through tunnels, around several hairpins, passing waterfalls and stunning backdrops, to our café lunch. This was great - the only café in this tiny village, with its own drinking water spring, and 26 people in identical dress, laughing and eating in the shade. The end was in sight, and I for one was getting a bit giddy...

After lunch, there was another 20 mile drop down from the plateau towards the coast, and this was our very last gently sweeping, snaking descent, through lovely scenery and on quiet smooth roads. I would definitely miss this once it was over. We had a headwind, so were able to pedal slowly in top gear, and maintain a pretty fast pace but with little effort. In the UK I've never encountered terrain like we'd seen in the last few days, and despite finding the climbing a challenge, I had loved the feeling of freedom as we whizzed down the hills, the wind in our faces and the sunshine on our backs. I was beginning to feel sad that it would be a while until we experienced this kind of cycling again.

From out of nowhere, a stiff climb loomed, and I asked Alberto for a little push. The heat was intense, I swear I could smell the sea, and I really didn't want to struggle for the last few miles. Once up the steepest bit, the traffic began to build, as we were obviously on the outskirts of civilisation and the sprawling expanse of the suburbs of Nice. Alberto now took the lead, to help us navigate the hectic streets, and we soon found Trevor and Vicky who had pulled off the road to check their route notes. It seemed quite fitting that our last stretch would be cycled together with the couple who had become firm friends in such a short time.

As we all followed Alberto like sheep, through the unfamiliar traffic lights, roundabouts and busy junctions, my mind switched off from the navigation, and began racing through a whirlwind of emotions. I had looked forward to completing this trip for five years, and now it was all but finished. I flashed through images from the last two weeks: from the horrendous weather at times, to the laughter and camaraderie with the cyclists in the evenings: from the breathtaking scenes of the Ardeche and Verdon gorges, to the picturesque villages and empty roads: from making it up

Ventoux and my hug with Bob at the top, to the giggles with Vicky over our most private anatomy: and to Mum and Dad and how much they would have enjoyed our recounting the trip, showing them pictures and maps, and how proud they'd have been. But most of all I felt so lucky to have shared this all with Bob. It simply wouldn't have been the same without him, and I was grateful that he'd been with me for every turn of my pedals. Now there were just a couple of miles left...

And there it was – the Mediterranean Sea! Following the others blindly, I hadn't realised where we were until the street we were on opened out onto the Nice promenade, and beyond it, the sea stretched out to the horizon. Again, the claps and cheers sounded from the others as we arrived at the bar which was our meeting point, and now I could no longer hold back the tears. All of the cyclists gave us hugs, congratulations, handshakes and grins, each one just as pleased with their own achievement as I was, and I can honestly say that I've never been hugged by so many sweaty men and women. Isabelle (who wasn't sweaty!) found me and gave me the warmest embrace and special words of congratulations, then held my hands in hers and asked "no regrets?", my only one being that I couldn't call Dad. Bob and I managed a quiet moment together. We were both crying and laughing, so pleased with what we'd done as 'Team Cullen', not needing to say anything, just knowing that we were both thinking the same - Mum and Dad had been with us every inch of the way.

But the celebrations weren't yet over. We all headed for the beach, where Isabelle and Alberto poured fizz into plastic cups for us all to shout 'cheers' in Icelandic, and to have our team photo by the sea. A few of them did the very British thing of taking off shoes and socks and paddling up to their ankles, but Isabelle and Alberto led the way straight in, followed by a couple of our braver companions. Alberto crept up behind me and said 'do you want a push now Jane?', and how could I refuse him, after he'd been such a help! So I was in, fully clothed and still grinning like a Cheshire cat.

With thighs like Chris Hoy, a bum like a baboon, and a million happy memories, I'd cycled coast-to-coast, the Channel to the Med, the entire length of France (well, 34 miles short!), and I was incredibly happy.

It's All Over

Dripping wet, smiling and proud, we still had another seven miles to cycle to our hotel, mostly along La Promenade des Anglais at Nice, looking at yachts which cost more money than most people can dream of, past the airport with its array of private jets on show, and all of humankind parading out in their finery. Once at our final destination, it really did feel like it was all over, as everyone's thoughts turned towards the practicalities of getting home. Bikes were to be stripped, labelled and left with Dylan and Alberto for them to pack into the vans to take back to the UK. Instead of laying out our cycling kit for the next day, we instead got out passports, boarding passes and made sure our luggage was travel-ready. A hive of activity, but with a very different mind-set.

We met Trevor and Vicky, and made our way to the restaurant for the 'last supper' with all our fellow cyclists. Before we ate, Isabelle stood to thank us all and handed out certificates, along with a brief speech about each and every one of us. She summed us all up perfectly! I had volunteered to make the reply - I felt better qualified than most to talk about the three tour guides, as Bob and I had spent much more time with Alberto and Dylan riding sweep at the back than any of the others, and of course, my fellow Mancunian Isabelle and I were quite well acquainted too.

I can't really remember exactly what I said as it was a blur of noise and white wine, but I hope I got the message across that we were grateful they had all worked so hard to make our lives as cyclists very easy. Our luggage was always waiting in our rooms when we arrived anywhere, the brew-stops and picnic lunches worked like clockwork, our bikes were miraculously fixed when anything went wrong, our safety and enjoyment had been their priority, and there was always a warm and welcoming smile, even when they probably felt little to smile about. Isabelle seemed genuinely pleased that I had made the speech, and not left it to one of the blokes.

Nice is a very busy city, and the few of us who chose to find a bar for a nightcap afterwards were soon separated in the melee of crowded streets, and so Bob and I headed back to the hotel. In the garden were the three tour guides, enjoying the cool of the evening before they retired. We sat with them for a while, drinking lukewarm rosé wine from our Peak Tours mugs, reminiscing about the last two weeks and talking about what comes next - a wonderful end to a most memorable holiday.

Total Miles – 881   (I did 847!)
Total Ascent – 67,128ft
Average Speed – 10.77mph
Total Calories – 46,513

Life Goes On

After the initial euphoria upon our return, regaling tales of our adventure to anyone who showed the remotest interest, life felt a little flat. We were straight back on our bikes as soon as my backside recovered sufficiently to slip onto the saddle, but I found myself whingeing "It's not quite France, is it?" at the rough roads, inconsiderate drivers, and overgrown hedgerows blocking the view. I also began some serious research into options for a new saddle...

I had more tests at the hospital which showed that I didn't have angina. My problem was probably respiratory, which would mean a different department and another waiting list, but my ticker is clearly quite healthy, and I really wish I'd known that before the trip.

Very soon reality began to kick in, and our trip was no longer the main focus for my mind or my conversation. There were just six weeks until Rebecca and James's wedding, and preparations were pretty much finished - although the final dress fitting, seating plans etc were a very welcome diversion from our everyday routine. Cameron finished his job at Wells and moved back in with us temporarily, whilst he got everything organised for his departure to Yale, and it felt good to have him home.

As the week of the wedding arrived, the excitement began to build, and with all the guests having to travel, most were treating themselves to a long weekend or mini-break arranged around the big day. St Andrews seemed to be teeming with friends and family for days, and it felt like the party had already started! Rebecca and James were relaxed and happy in the knowledge that everything was running smoothly, and all that remained was to turn up on time.

Their wedding day could not have been better. It was everything they had imagined but with the added bonus of clear blue skies. It was the most magical setting, centred on the university quad with its carefully manicured lawn surrounded by college buildings steeped in history. The university chapel runs along one side of the quad, with the sun streaming in colourful dapples through the ancient stained glass, and the arched cloisters providing the perfect backdrop for photos.

Every father dreams of walking their daughter down the aisle, and Bob was no exception. As a proud Scot he wore a kilt and relished every step of the way, only allowing the emotion to take over as he lifted her veil when they reached James at the front of the church. Rebecca looked stunning, and it was lovely to watch them both beam with happiness throughout the day. Cameron was best man, and also played a flute solo during the service – a rare chance for family and friends to hear him perform. The reception was equally memorable, in the building just across the lawn, the party spilling out into the gardens in the sunshine, and the dancefloor was packed with smiling revellers throughout the whole of the evening. It was the perfect day from beginning to end, and as Bob said in his speech, it was the obvious place for a girl born in Scotland on St Andrews day; who went to St Andrews University; and who said 'yes' to James on St Andrews beach; to tie the knot.

As we travelled home a couple of days later, coming down from our 'high', my thoughts turned to Cameron's looming departure in two weeks' time. Whilst I was incredibly proud and happy for him to have the opportunity to study with one of the flute world's leading names, Yale is a long, long way away. I very much wanted him to go, spread his wings fully, embrace a whole new life and culture, but I really didn't look forward to waving him off, and I tried really hard not to be the embarrassing blubbering wreck at the airport. As soon as term began, his schedule was hectic, but it was lovely to be able to talk to him via Skype, and when we flew out to visit him in the autumn, we could see that he was flourishing in his new environment. He definitely had an exciting and rewarding two years ahead.

Last year had been my annus horribilis when we lost Mum and Dad, but this year had been the polar opposite. The cycle training, the epic ride through France, Rebecca and James's wonderful wedding weekend, and Cameron settling into his adventure in Yale, had meant we'd been on cloud 9 for months. Life was about to seem a little dull, or maybe it was time to plan another bike ride...?

Epilogue

When I finished LeJog, I had such a rush of pride and an enormous sense of achievement. For some strange reason, Channel to the Med was different. Rather than feeling I'd completed a challenge, ticked a box, I felt I had discovered a whole new world and found places that I never knew existed until I was right there breathing them in. It's hard to believe that some of the most awe-inspiring places in the world are just a bike ride away - literally on our doorstep. Instead of fuelling my desire for another goal, I felt a thirst for discovery, and a need to explore more of what I have had the good fortune to experience. What will live in my memory forever is not the scaling of Ventoux, or the hailstorms, nor puffing up the hills or the banter with my fellow cyclists.

What will be permanently etched on my mind are the D-Day veterans watching with pride as the Pegasus Bridge opened; the exhilaration I felt on our first really long descent through Alpine-esque scenery; the scent of bergamot and calls of cuckoos as we passed through some of France's most remote countryside; the simple beauty of the poppies which welcomed us along the entire route; the magnificent churches perched high on hillsides and clifftops; the breath-taking gorges of the Ardeche and Verdon, and especially the late afternoon's ride as we followed the Verdon upstream; and the peaceful warmth of the sea washing over me as I floated in my cycling gear. We could sign up with Peak Tours and cycle another of their amazing adventures (and we probably will), but I doubt that any other will be quite so humbling and rewarding. Five years in the making, but this truly was the trip of a lifetime.

I started this book thinking that mine had not been a remarkable life, but in pouring my soul onto paper, I have realised that it has, and that it only really began when I met Bob. Together we have achieved and experienced more than I would have dared to dream. Who knows what lies ahead, but as 'Team Cullen', it will no doubt be an adventure.

Printed in Great Britain
by Amazon